SALMON

*Diverse Voices from Ireland
and the World*

Well, You Don't Look It!

Women Writers in Ireland Reflect on Ageing

Edited by

Éilís Ní Dhuibhne and Michaela Schrage-Früh

Published in 2024 by
Salmon Poetry
Cliffs of Moher, County Clare, Ireland
Reprinted in 2024 by
Salmon Poetry
Website: www.salmonpoetry.com
Email: info@salmonpoetry.com

ISBN 978-1-915022-60-8

Cover Image: 'Maybe I Will' by Brigid O'Brien
Cover Design & Typesetting: Siobhán Hutson

Printed in Ireland by Sprint Print

Salmon Poetry gratefully acknowledges the support of
The Arts Council / An Chomhairle Ealaíon

He who is silent is taken to agree;
he ought to have spoken when he was able to.
                                        —Latin Proverb

In the middle of the road I had a stone
I had a stone in the middle of the road.
                              —Carlos Drummond de Andrade

Contents

Michaela Schrage-Früh   *Introduction*

'Well, you don't look it!' – These words are usually meant as a compliment, especially when directed at a woman 'of a certain age'. And what woman wouldn't be gratified by such a flattering remark? It is only when we take a moment to reflect on why it is that a youthful appearance should be so desirable that the more sinister meanings of the praise most of us have given or received will dawn on us: ageing women are not valued highly in western society; they'd better hide their age to adhere to societal standards that tend to conflate 'beauty' or 'novelty' with 'youth' and that can render women 'past their prime' largely invisible. Youthful looks in older women also conform to the mantra of positive or active ageing, which – in line with neoliberal ideas of self-reliance – suggests that people who fall ill or show outward signs of ageing may somehow be to blame for not being active or positive enough – regardless of social, economic, genetic, and other factors. The phrase/praise (and similar ones like 'looking good for one's age'; 'ageing gracefully' etc.) also shines a light on the gendered dimension of ageing: while men are often said to age like 'fine wine', women tend to just get 'old'. Which is not to say that older men don't grapple with their share of ageist stereotypes, the figures of the 'grumpy' or 'dirty' old man being cases in point. And yet, the 'double standard of ageing'[1], as diagnosed by Susan Sontag in 1972, still very much holds true in this day and age: Women's ageing still tends to be judged more relentlessly than men's, and, to use Margaret M. Gullette's phrase, women are 'aged by culture'[2] sooner than their male peers; with 50, the age around which most women go through the menopause, still considered a significant turning point.

In recent years the theme of women's ageing has been addressed more openly, with, for instance, the 'novel of ripening' or the 'menopause novel' becoming literary genres in their own right that typically feature female protagonists in later life. In popular culture, there is a trend towards older women models or social media 'influencers' that may serve as positive role models for either 'ageing gracefully' or its opposite. Increasingly, too, we see nuanced older characters starring in films and TV shows, such as retired school teacher Nancy Stokes (portrayed by Emma Thompson in her sixties) who explores her mature sexuality with a significantly younger partner in

---

[1] Susan Sontag, "The Double Standard of Aging", Saturday Review, 1972. 31. *NZ.org: Periodicals, Books and Authors*. http://www.unz.org/Pub/SaturdayRev-1972sep23-00029

[2] Margaret M. Gullette, *Aged by Culture* (Chicago: The University of Chicago Press, 2004).

Good Luck to You, Leo Grande (2022) or *Grace and Frankie* (embodied by Jane Fonda and Lily Tomlin in their late seventies/early eighties), who discover the world of sex toys and age-friendly toilet seats while celebrating female friendship and entrepreneurship. And more and more women focus on the losses and gains of growing older in memoirs, essays, and other forms of life writing. In Ireland the theme of ageing has been addressed in both poetry and fiction by women, pioneeringly so by Eavan Boland (1944-2020), who from the late 1980s onwards wrote poems against the silences surrounding women's ageing, noting in her poem 'Anna Liffey' that 'an ageing woman finds no shelter in language', while also poignantly allowing her lyrical persona to discover that: 'I was a voice'[3]. Surprisingly though, the present compilation is the first anthology of Irish writing devoted solely to older women's voices in life writing, poetry, and short fiction.

The idea for this anthology emerged from a research project titled 'Restorying Ageing: Older Women and Life Writing' (2021-2022), funded by the Irish Research Council and conducted by a group of researchers at the University of Galway in partnership with Age & Opportunity. At the heart of the project was the idea that 'older' women are rarely heard or seen in public discourse, that old age tends to render women invisible. We were wondering how women aged 50 and over felt about popular representations of older women in the media, if they could recognize themselves and their own lives in such representations, and if life writing might be a way to challenge, complicate and 'restory' those stereotypical images that still often dominate public discourse. Might life writing in its myriad manifestations be a way for older women to insert their personal, lived experiences into broader social and cultural discourses, thereby effecting positive change? Margaret M. Gullette's concept of 'critical age autobiography'[4] suggests that it is possible to challenge cultural stereotypes about ageing by countering them with individual stories. In a similar vein, age studies scholar Ruth E. Ray emphasizes the need to move 'beyond positions in which one has been 'storied' by others to positions in which one reflects, reconsiders, modifies, rewrites, and 'restories' oneself'. In restorying themselves, older women might thus be empowered to resist 'the cultural forces that attempt to story [their] lives, especially in terms of age, throughout the life course'[5].

---

[3] Eavan Boland, "Anna Liffey", *Collected Poems* (Manchester: Carcanet, 1995), 199-205.

[4] Margaret Morganroth Gullette, *Declining to Decline: Cultural Combat and the Politics of the Midlife* (Charlottesville, VA: University Press of Virginia, 1997), 220.

[5] Ruth E. Ray, *Beyond Nostalgia: Aging and Life-Story Writing* (Charlottesville and London: University Press of Virginia, 2000), 28, 30.

The 'Restorying Ageing' project consisted of two phases: the first involved two focus group sessions with women aged between 50 and 80, all of them Irish residents. In the first online meeting, this group was presented with visual representations of older women, including TV ads, media images, and video clips from both Irish and broader Anglophone contexts. The participants were then invited to respond to these images as well as to questions designed by the research team. In the second online meeting the same group discussed excerpts from life writing by older women, including memoir, poetry, essays, and tweets, which they had read prior to the meeting. In the second phase, some of the focus group participants attended a creative life writing workshop led by Éilís Ní Dhuibhne. Their creative assignments were partly based on texts discussed in the focus groups, ranging from poems by Jenny Joseph and Paula Meehan to excerpts from life writing by Nuala O'Faolain and Penelope Lively. A selection of their creative outputs is compiled here alongside commissioned and reprinted works by established writers.

All contributors included in this anthology are based in – or have a clear biographical connection to – Ireland, both North and South. Their age ranges from their early fifties to their early eighties, thus comprising a heterogeneous group of 'older women' spanning several generations. In assembling their creative texts, we have decided against chronological, thematic or alphabetical order, instead opting for an arrangement that places the fictional stories at the centre, framed by alternating poems and reflective essays that depict the diversity of themes, perspectives, and modes in all its dazzling and unpredictable array.

Ageing is a mixed bag. Many of the texts compiled here are haunted by a sense of loss; a childhood and youth irrevocably gone unless conjured up in reminiscence or dreams; a past still lingering with us in memories of our former selves and dead loved ones; the spectre of death looming as the inevitable endpoint of our journey through life, harder to ignore as we grow older. Time passing, grief, and fear of illness and death are recurring themes throughout the collection. The anthology also includes poems, reflections and stories about the hardships of older age caused by ill health, infirmity, caring responsibilities, and financial strain. It offers reflections about the isolation, plight, and unjust treatment experienced by many older people (men and women alike) during the Covid-19 pandemic. These pieces testify to the manifold ways in which we are 'aged by culture' as much as to the pressing need for political and social change when it comes to creating viable futures for an ageing demographic; a demographic which ultimately comprises every generation's future.

Yet there is also a tangible sense of appreciation for what one contributor calls 'this gift of age': the celebratory joy of living in the moment, as well as the unbridled anticipation of an exciting future, things yet to come, still to be experienced; envisioning newly found freedoms, with older age a time to 'wear purple / with a red hat that doesn't go'[6] and greeting the unexpected with humour that turns even a walk to the hospital into 'another great adventure'; cherishing the happiness of lasting or new connections with others – friends, spouses, lovers, adult children, grandchildren but also writers, past and present; a sense of amazement, resilience, creativity, and purpose; making the most of the 'harvested riches' that old age can bring. Time and again the contributors invoke nature, and seasonal change in particular, as a prism through which to view ageing: the seasons may influence how 'old' we feel, but they are cyclical, defying chronological age, promising renewal and growth. There is a sense of 'becoming' as older women explore their new identities and roles as grandmothers, writers, retirees, travellers, 'mature' lovers, and more.

What all the contributions have in common is that they defy easy categorization and stereotypical representation. They explore ageing from within, charting new territory and reporting on it 'with a certain authority', from the vantage point of someone who is 'a native now' and knows 'what goes on here'[7]. We hope that the rich 'reports' on later life compiled in this anthology will resonate with readers across genders and generations and that they will contribute to an emerging discourse on the lived realities of ageing, and its imaginative possibilities, in Ireland and beyond.

[6] Jenny Joseph, "Warning". 1961. https://www.scottishpoetrylibrary.org.uk/poem/warning/
[7] Penelope Lively, *Ammonites and Leaping Fish: A Life in Time* (Fig Tree, 2013), 3.

Ann Ingle

Reflections of an Older Woman

I will be 84 in August. It's a sure sign of ageing when you start declaring your age unprompted. It might be because I hope to hear, 'well, you don't look it', or perhaps it's just a sense of pride for having made it this far.

I live with my youngest daughter, her husband and their three children and I am so grateful for my intergenerational way of living. It makes life easy. I don't have to do the shopping, wash the clothes or clean the house. While this is wonderful, on bad days a feeling of uselessness sometimes comes over me. I sit with my smartphone at breakfast and finish Wordle and the New York Times mini-crossword and look at the empty page in my diary. I hate those empty pages. I like to see something there, even if it is only a doctor's appointment.

My housemates conscientiously urge me to take 'my walk' and that is so good of them. Sometimes, I just don't feel like it and reluctantly push myself out the door.

Walking has never been my thing. If I have somewhere to go I have no problem, pain in the hip or not, but it's the mindless meandering around that gets to me. For long walks, I abandon my stick and use my new walking aid, a rollator. It's a very swish affair and the other day a fellow older woman passing by called after me 'I like your wheels'.

It's a Swedish design called Swift, not that I go at a rapid rate but I can dream. It is a great help to me in navigating the pavements of Phibsborough, my eyes not being so good. I have macular degeneration which is treated with injections every eight weeks.

My earphones are part of my ensemble. I listen to novels all the time and that is a joy and a distraction. So, with great works of art ringing in my ears and a steady grip on my new best Swedish friend, I walk out every day and might be gone for an hour if rain doesn't stop play. I always survey my surroundings when I go to new places in case of trip hazards and if the pavements are icy I never venture out.

Recently I had no problem walking to the Mater hospital, calling over my shoulder to my daughter who was pulling my little case, 'another great adventure'.

I had been diagnosed with breast cancer and was about to have my left breast removed. It never occurred to me that a woman of my age would require a mastectomy. I thought it only occurred in younger women but according to Breast Care Ireland, 36% of breast cancer is diagnosed in women over 70.

The operation left me cancer free and ready to get on with life, albeit at a leisurely pace. I am a proponent of slow living. I don't rush. A steady pace is essential to avoid the dreaded falls. I learned that the hard way. Climbing steps to reach something is out of the question. And heavy kettles. And pouring water into a glass can result in disaster because of my wonky eyes.

There are many things you give up doing in your 80s. Hiking up mountains, not that I was ever very fond of that, is out of the question. But you would imagine a simple thing like putting on a pair of tights would be straightforward enough. Not any more. I struggled for ages the other day to get the second leg in and gave up in frustration. No more tights for me.

I feel nostalgic when I remember the excitement of the first pair of tights I bought in Madame Nora's in O'Connell Street. It doesn't matter. I can wear trousers and go bare legged when the weather gets warmer.

I don't care anyway. I don't think anyone really looks at me anymore. Peggy Seeger's song *The Invisible Woman* says it all:

> *I can't recall when it first happened,*
> *don't know how I became so unseen,*
> *when my tangible self was put on the shelf*
> *these words on the label: has been.*

Yesterday I went out wearing earrings that didn't match. They were the same earrings but in different colours, one bright red and the other midnight blue. (I bought two pairs because I couldn't decide which colour I liked the best and then lost one of each of them). Nobody noticed my mismatched earrings. Invisible woman, you see?

Anyway, I have decided I like the look and will continue to wear them on occasion to spice things up. There is an upside to not being noticed. It gives me a sense of freedom as Jenny Joseph puts it so well in her wonderful poem *Warning*, if I feel like it:

> *I shall go out in my slippers in the rain*
> *And pick flowers in other people's gardens*
> *And learn to spit.*

I am free to do as much as my old body allows. There is no job to go to, no children to mind and no responsibilities. I could sit and watch television all day if I wanted to, but it hasn't come to that yet.

And would you believe, my opinion and advice is sought after on rare occasions. I find this gratifying even if it is only a daughter asking how to cook tandoori chicken or looking for the best recipe for sweet shortcrust pastry (225g plain flour, 150g chilled butter, 25g icing sugar and 1 large egg, all whizzed up together). Two of my sons, invariably ring me at Christmas looking for my stuffing recipe. Not sure if they are just trying to humour me or if they really forget from year to year how to do it.

If you are lucky enough to live as long as I have, the sad fact is your circle of friends grows smaller. I make a point of meeting up with the friends that remain as often as I can. Before we get into our lunch we have the 'organ recital'. That's what Maeve Binchy used to call it. We recite our ailments and recount hospital appointments and then quickly move on to more important matters like the state of the nation and our families.

Spending time with the grandchildren is one of the great joys of my life. They don't expect anything from me. I'm not invisible to them. Being a grandmother to 18 young people is a privilege. I play games and read stories to the younger ones and try to impart wisdom to the older ones. I want them all to know that kindness, love and gratitude are what matters most in our lives. That holy trinity will see us through at any age.

Paula Meehan

The Hands

Today I got my old woman's hands.
I laid my young woman's hands away
in the drawer with my young woman's hair,
that thick dark braid that hung to my waist.
Mind how he swung me once round and round
the garden, to Sergeant Pepper's Band.
That was long ago, a wedding day.
The ring is lost; lost are all my cares.
Old woman's hands now, old woman's face.

from *Geomantic* (Dublin: Dedalus Press, 2016)

Rita Ann Higgins

This Day I was Older

Pain on wakening, my shoulders, down my legs.
This day I was older. I reached for my phone.
Pain was a fat ten, I took my hand back.
Phones are overrated.
Washing my hair -pain was a twelve
hair washing was overrated.
Then the bra straps – yada yada,
bras are overrated.

In no time
I was a scruffy braless crank
with PMR to my name.
Old age was snapping,
then along came steroids
and I didn't need a broom.
I was always hungry.
Things that shouldn't go went -
caramelised onion and sweet cake.

Eighteen months the steroids sentence-
enough time to strip the goodness from your bones
We'll taper you off them when the time comes.
I don't think you really 'have it' the man says.
I tapered down and down the rabbit hole of clinic visits.
Then one day I was tapered.
You are now a tapered woman
and there is nowhere to hide.

Time was no healer,
it passed me like a raging train
on the brink of an assault.
Old killjoy inflammation
came back and landed on my love handles
making me walk funny.

My gait was no longer mine.
I couldn't pick me out of a walking line up
if I had to walk that line.
Bursitis the man says
the man always knows.

Try aqua aerobics, try a foam roller
walk further, do it faster.
Never turn around, keep your beak facing north.
Nowadays I surf around the landing
on my foam-roller, never naked it must be said.
Sometimes I wear an old leather pants -
just for pig iron.

I'm afraid of the aqua aerobics group
I see them in the pool
they will devour me. I will sink.
The walking I can do
with someone else's walk.
I never go anywhere
without my free travel pass.
I walk so far then I hop on a bus,
maybe hop is a bit of a boast-

I get to there and I'll walk
most of the way home.
Anything to be carried has to go on my back
I wear a small haversack -the pilgrims progress.
Sometimes my shoulders act the maggot
but never on feast days or holy days of
subjugation.

Currently, I have a solitary gall stone
as big as mortal sin-
otherwise my gallbladder is unremarkable.
That has to come out, the man says.
Until then I foam-roll on the landing
I walk faster and further
I never look back.

Mary O'Donnell

The Growing Button

When our daughter was five, she used occasionally feel overwhelmed by the act of growing, by change itself, when she sometimes had to do things she wasn't ready for. So, we used to tell her she had an invisible gadget just above her belly-button, a Growing Button. All we had to do was tap lightly, and it would stop. Stopping the Growing Button was an occasional ruse that allowed a child who felt she was being hurried along too quickly, to take a psychological pause. It worked.

Now, decades on and older, *I* wouldn't mind, on occasion, being able to halt my own 'button', my proud, still mentally energetic, growing *old* button, as I hurry along, not always ready for what presents itself. Sure, I've adjusted to the social web of intricate standards, where so much needs to be bargained with, treated with a certain delicacy and discretion, and can't automatically be taken at face value. I've seen how all of us reflect different truths about reality towards one another. But there are moments when I too, as once my daughter, wish I could stop the clock.

Perhaps I hear a fabulous piece of music, live or on radio, or I go someplace and realise I'll never return to that place in that moment, and most poignant of all, I see a young couple madly in love with one another and know that the time for ardour on that level has passed and become something else, something different. What I feel is pure grief—concealed, sometimes joked about—but nonetheless grief. Something has passed. Something is over.

I'm a little like eleventh century King Canute, who, attempting to demonstrate to those around him that the King was not divine, brought his throne to the beach and ordered the incoming tide to turn back on itself. After failing to hold back the tide, so the legend goes, he removed his crown, hung it from a crucifix and never wore it again.

Perhaps the struggle with age is mostly a question of humanist pride rather than Canute's challenge to divinity. We're full of it, drenched with it in ourselves and how we wish to live and be, and this particular 'deadly sin' may be one of the hardest to relinquish. Pride allows me to deceive myself on certain days that I haven't really changed so much in the past two decades, that although I'm not young, I remain youthful. But who am I kidding?

The outspoken, frank and analytical commentator-philosopher Susan Sontag, writing the eponymously titled essay 'The Double Standard of Ageing' (1972), tackled the social convention—still alive and well—by which ageing is seen to enhance some men while progressively diminishing most women.

Those of us with men in our lives know all too well that, in different circumstances, the guys aged 65+ could probably find a partner at least twenty years younger than they, but the corollary doesn't apply. An older woman with a thirty or forty-something man? Rarely. Maybe never, apart from Brigitte Macron.

But to some extent, Sontag, who suffered viciously from diminishing cancer treatments, was misguided. The lens through which she viewed the problem was, in this essay, based on the question of desirability, rather than on questions to do with time and how to spend it while one's health holds up. A beauty, compelling to both men and women, she cared about desirability.

The question of just what confirms or denies female desirability is interesting. In later life, oestrogen levels have plummeted, and consequently, the subliminal signals emitted by the subconscious body and mind have also vanished. No amount of HRT can replace these. On the plus side for some of us, hormonal deficit contributes to the invisibility others among us complain about. Frankly, there are times when I find physical invisibility a bonus: you walk into a room and nobody glances a second time. You are a shape, a person, but your mystery and fascination are now as neutral as water. That's okay. Self-consciousness vanishes, and for good.

For me, the 'problem' of ageing has more to do with increasing reminders that my body is no longer what it was, that like a once-gleaming ceramic urn it has succumbed to cracks in the glaze, a few pieces chipped off or missing, and a general air of incipient autumn-on-the-verge-of-winter. Then I ask myself how could it be a problem when it's simply part of the passage from womb to tomb, as natural as the growth, flowering and decline of a tree? Sometimes, I sense that bones, ligaments, muscles, skin, all my organs, are either quiescent and doing nothing much (ovaries, womb), or else doing too much of what they shouldn't (heart, kidneys, bones). Yet, having had a throat to abdomen CT Scan a few years ago, I'll never forget the intricate beauty of (on the screen and image by image) sighting my internal self going about its business and at work, magnificently complex, a cosmos in micro.

I realised that age didn't sully what's beneath the skin, or need not if one is more or less healthy. Although fear is a factor throughout all of life for many of us, the contemporary, fashionable, focus on 'mindfulness' doesn't do much for me. I'm not interested in 'living in the moment' either, because my inner self imagines it's still young and aspires, rather young-goatishly, to a future in which things happen, exciting things that interest me and allow me to buzz intellectually and emotionally. I treasure the time left in which to make poems, novels, investigate ideas, and know all too well that in say, 15 – 20 years' time, the literary landscape I'm still a part of will have eclipsed me and my like more or less completely.

The truth is, sometimes I've had to concede both my talent and time because of choices made: caring roles, partner roles, the life-long intimate parsing of the sensitive democracy we call marriage, which is paradoxically beautiful, when viewed as an ongoing, meaningful dialogue between two people. Few of us are geniuses though we've all occasionally enjoyed moments of what we imagine is 'genius'. The paradox continues: I now feel freer than ever to deviate from rigid writing plans, the savage edge softened on some of my ambition, and as a result I experience much, much more than I did before.

But sometimes a day comes when a person wakes up and those elements and structures have vanished. One is widowed. One divorces. Or a couple stay together but the interaction has shifted like tectonic plates now grinding over one another after years of accommodating one another. Or, quite simply, one is alone and with a failing memory. That novel you read with such intensity only a month before, is already becoming thready in recall. Aloneness isn't necessarily lonely. Aloneness means the mind can be liberated from petty concerns, like a long and expanding plain over which a canopy of stars beckon, and the airs are benign. Now, perhaps for the first time, there is time. On one's hands. In one's head. Around one's body. How wonderful, even with a tendency to forget names!

Younger women complain about lack of time, especially when they become parents. This may be a result of huge pressures on them to do with getting it right, being good mothers. How cruel to yet another generation of women, entrapped by the biological imperative for some of their most prime years. I always know that when a young woman writer becomes pregnant, it will (for most) bring a considerable pause in her output and visible creativity. I've seen it, I've been through it, and I still observe it around me. Now though, my relative calmness in the face of their situation amazes me. What younger women don't know, and what will face many of them, is the future care of their own parents, who live into their 90s and beyond. And that's much harder, given the ambiguous and weird attitude official Ireland radiates towards the truly vulnerable old.

If I could stop my own 'growing button' right now, what would I want? I would want not to weaken physically. I would want strong, undented-by-osteopenia bones, I'd want to be able to jump—I'm not so good at that any more—and keep up at a Zumba class, and use a skipping rope for five full minutes. I think I might wish for a generally more physical life, in a sunnier climate. But the truth is, those are just wistful dreams about the might-have-beens, and I don't bother about those so much.

I'm happy enough as long as I can move. As Clarissa Pinkóla Estes famously wrote in *Women who Run with the Wolves* (1989), *What moves cannot freeze*. I've never forgotten those four words, true in every sense. They apply now that I've grown older, now time works with my body to bring me to sacred earth eventually. We can choose to see death as something fearful or something natural. When both my parents died, I was conscious of them ebbing like an outgoing tide into the most natural pattern as their souls pulled away from the quotidian, from the trifling, from the multiple fears of this world.

Our 'Growing Buttons' never stop. They grow us up, and then they grow us back down again. But only when the work is complete. Or what I think of, philosophically, as *my* work, which I still need to do with, I hope, integrity. So far, I feel: gratitude, occasional fear, occasional anxiety, and dancing, sunlit motes of hope, that all will work out in the most natural way possible, as I crack on, daily, towards the inevitable.

Helena Nolan

One Hundred Poems About The Menopause

Why are there not one hundred poems about the menopause?
Women are more than half the population, after all
And those of us with luck enough to live beyond a half-life
Which is still a lot, despite so many efforts to deny -
Will surely wish to see those lives reflected in a line

See our fates in the mirrored halls of poetry, stanza'd rooms
Where all our days play out, like well-sung tunes
From dancing gals, to tarts, to toothless crones
And all the other tropes that tread the boards
Ah yes...the well-worn shoes and worn-out heels and hose

The down-turned mouths, the lips, like purses, torn
And bleeding, scorned and emptied, missing vowels
The emptied vessels, flustered faces, addled brains
And more, flush, flash, de-fleshed, the knuckles strung
With ropes of shrivelled veins, all ripe for symbols

Metaphor, fair game, flushed, flashed and barren
Cackled with disdain, the witch, the bitch
The invisible ditch in which she ends her days...
But that would be a shame – sing instead of a second life
The glow of a second age, of rage, of intellect and artistry

Of a new domain, bled on the sharp tooth of experience
Lit by the bright eye of age, that sees through obstacles, round corners
Through the bloodshot dark of war, through all the bloodied histories
To herstory, past birth and death and agonies of both, past sheets
Past picking up the pieces, cups and saucers, china, bone

Moving onwards, forwards, upwards, always towards today
One hundred poems about the menopause -
One hundred and one hundred and one hundred more
Past pausing time, stretched taut, set sail across the longest
Proudest page, one hundred thousand waves, against the shore

Eileen Casey

Mirabilis Jalapa (The Four O'Clock Flower)

'Twilight years', 'Over the hill', 'Past it', or even 'Long in the tooth'. Worn out terms describing older age, some less kind than others. In his famous poem 'At Grass', Philip Larkin uses the image of race horses retired from the winner's enclosure as a metaphor for the dwindling power of the British Empire. Horses who once knew 'cups and stakes and handicaps'. Larkin's opening lines:

> 'The eye can hardly pick them out
> From the cold shade they shelter in'

strike a chord however when it comes to referencing our older population. I know from whence I speak, reaching the grand age of three score and seven this coming August. I use the quote from Larkin's poem because I too have sheltered in that 'cold shade'. At least in some areas of my life. Not all, but some.

Take ordinary day-to-day living. My husband John and I are both retired. We have arrived at parental utopia (children grown and flown), a state we visualised when young, exhausted primary carers. Parental utopia means leisurely days with nothing to do and all day to do it. No responsibilities, only to ourselves. An attractive proposition while in the throes of rearing a boisterous brood. Morning cuppas gulped instead of sipped. Milk sloshed over cereal bowls, lunches packed into schoolbags. John rushing out, hoping our jalopy will start. Especially on icy mornings, rooftops shrouded with snow, the engine choking and spluttering to life. I'd hold my breath, our youngest cradled in one arm while I warmed up her feed. Then later, husband home from the fray, I went out to work, packing shelves in a local supermarket. I was part of the first 'night-packer' team in the country, a job I managed to keep going for eight years. So of course, the luxury of not having such an energetic lifestyle seemed appealing. Until grandchildren came along and before we knew it, we're plunged back 'there' again, albeit being able to return them (most of the time). 'Helping out,' in this regard also has a sell-by date. Unfortunately, I see a lot of grandparents looking tired and drained, purely because childcare is just so expensive. John and I 'stood our watch' as the saying goes, taking care of our own family, then looking after little ones while their parents worked. But the day comes when the strain begins to bite. That youthful energy we once had in abundance doesn't last forever. All our fledglings are now in school and that situation's eased. It's a dilemma for grandparents because saying 'no' brings an avalanche of guilt. Grandparents are expected to be parental extensions, but if the energy's not there, it's not there. Good health in older age is not a guarantee either. Speaking of monetary necessity (mostly the reason parents work): after years of our combined labour, John and I find ourselves entitled to nothing. I receive the contributory pension but it's not much more than the non-contributory. When I applied for my pension, I was told my work record was exemplary but all those stamps, contributions to the system, is not reflected. Sometimes I wonder was it worth our while getting married, working so hard etc. We pay private health insurance, keep a car on the road and all the while the cost of living rises like a skyscraper. Non-contributory pension is not much less plus there's a whole raft of benefits that go with non-contributory which we cannot access.

I wake early as I've always done. I rarely stay in bed past 7.30 a.m. The habit of a lifetime. I listen for the birds, loving their sweet chirrups. I'll watch for a blackbird or a jaunty robin on our plum tree, glorious in pale pink flower. When it sheds, the blossoms drift down like confetti, taking me back to my June wedding in 1977. I wore the dress my sister Mary made for me. Plain, simple yet elegant. John sleeps longer than I do. I'm careful not to disturb him. He's earned his rest, worked long hours, took on all the overtime he could. Our mortgage payments in the early years were almost three weeks of his monthly salary. I absolutely had to work. So, all these years later, I see families still struggling in this same situation. I worked evenings so childcare wasn't an issue but it was certainly tiring, working both sides of the day, burning the candle both ends.

John is the same weight he was on the day we married whereas I've plumped out. His hair is grey although he still has lots of it. It was raven black when we met. He cut a Heathcliff type figure, striding down Rathmines Road, flatland capital of Dublin. I worked in Heuston Station as a shorthand typist, one of the best skills I ever learnt. It served me well when I began writing, first as a hobby but then more seriously. Sometimes, looking back at photographs, how we once were, I'm inclined to feel some sadness. I accept there's no Tír na Nóg, no fountain of youth. On a bad day, catching sight of myself in a mirror, Sylvia Plath's words drift to me...

'Each morning it is her face that replaces the darkness.
In me she has drowned a young girl, and in me an old woman/
Rises toward her day after day, like a terrible fish'. (Mirror, 1961)

I mind but not to the extent that I'd undergo plastic surgery or tummy tucks or 'lifts' where flesh is 'loose'. Celebrities who say they are 'embracing' old age are mostly those who've had 'work done' and that's their right of course. Yet, good health is very attractive too and creates a glow no amount of money can buy. Lots of exercise is factored into my day. Long walks, even in the rain. Helen Mirren is a great role model. Growing older with grace and style. As is Judi Dench and lots more women of that vintage.

However, it's Samuel Beckett who sums up our daily routines. His 'ballast of the everyday'. When everything we do plays out in slow motion, even the smallest actions such as filling the kettle, plugging it in, waiting for water to boil, listening for the clink of metal against china as sugar is spooned then stirred. We don't wish to shrink the whole nine yards of the day too early. We eke it out rather than splurge. Without some level of being resourceful, courageous, optimistic, growing into the last segment of our life wheel can be challenging. Especially from the point of view of boredom. Unfortunately, there's no skip hire that will come and collect all those hours we have no need for. The ones after or before lunch, those ten minutes to turning on the radio for the latest global or national update. Quarter past pottering in the garden... weather permitting. Time is something we have plenty of, enough to hoard. Swallows build their nests from spit and clay. Yes, it takes hard work to stave off boredom because boredom has a domino effect. It literally paralyses which in turn affects confidence. Life is like a fairground ride. It slows down and speeds up. I accept that. If I want to 'shake' things up, then that's down to my efforts. I don't have a magic wand. Luckily, I live in South County Dublin, a county very much respectful of its ageing population. It has a vibrant arts community going back to the early 70s. Also, I thoroughly recommend the film 'Ordinary Love' (2019) starring Liam Neeson and Leslie Manville. With humour and grace, the ordinary lives of a couple are played out, against the backdrop of illness (Manville's character). What strikes me about the narrative is that it reflects the repetitive nature of day-to-day living as we age. We sometimes suppose that other ageing couples are 'living it up' and that we are out of kilter. This film helps me to realise the truth of the matter. Having a companion at this stage of my life is also a blessing. I can't imagine life without John and that is a scenario (should he predecease me) I'm not looking forward to.

Lock-down tested a lot of couples' relationships. Being cooped up with each other 24/7 meant a lot of 'stuff' came to the surface. A lifetime spent together generates plenty of issues. John and I are no different. He's a minimalist and I'm not. I won't go so far as to say I'm a consummate magpie but I have more regard for 'things' than he has. I've been warned. If I go before him, all my clutter will end up in a skip. We laugh about it but there's an edge to it. After all, someone will be left to deal with clutter, when I 'go'. Which brings me to the possibility itself. When I was 35 or so, I woke up one night very stressed. I dreamt I had passed away and I was terrified. The prospect of closing my eyes and being engulfed by darkness filled me with horror. I fully explored the whole idea of death, instead of pushing it away as I had done on numerous occasions, especially when my father died and then my mother. Strangely enough, when I allowed myself to fully experience these emotions, to embrace this inevitable prospect, the terror left me. My brother died last year. I am still in mourning for him but I celebrate his life rather than dwell on his illness and final days. We were close childhood pals. It's a downside of growing older that we lose siblings and friends. It's unavoidable. When my mother passed away, I found grief counselling extremely helpful.

Memories are like stepping stones and it's good to venture down 'Memory Lane'. Again, the phrase is just another construct and romanticised somewhat but reliving and reviving scenes and emotions from the past is important. All those tableaux vivants, those 'stills' can breathe again in memory. Happy times especially should be revisited. Written down if possible. These feelings are still within us. Hand them down to those who come after us. Keep a photographic record, documenting who's who on the back. Write snapshots of memory. Paying attention to them pays dividends. Use the one opening phrase repeatedly, 'I remember'... it can open a valuable storehouse treasury. The playwright Dennis Potter realised the power of memory. *Cold Lazarus* and *Karaoke*, his final works for the BBC are testimony. Recording memory is an enriching pursuit as I grow older. Excavating the past, respecting it, passing it on.

Ageing is about curating a life. When my grandchildren look at me, I don't want them just to see a woman who needs more than a few wrinkles ironed out (literally and figuratively), a woman whose hair is grey, whose hands are becoming bony and who is no longer running marathons (I have a few 'walking' marathons under my belt). I'd like them to see an intelligent, creative and engaging companion. I want to be like the *Mirabilis Jalapa*, a flower of many colours. Mirabilis (from scientific Latin meaning 'admirable') Jalapa is a night flowerer, crimson coloured, beginning to open in late afternoon, just as dusk is falling.

The Four O'Clock Flower

Unnoticed in daylight. Drab
petals fold stem tight. Forced
to bide your time, no clues
cue your presence. Plain
in pale sight. Morning
creeps by. Late afternoon
dims noon. You flare to life,

spot-lit by evening's crenulation,
scarlet flames around you.
Songbirds parachute down.
Drawn to *Mirabilis Jalapa*,
named when Aztecs ruled.
Miraculous revelation,
shadow lipped. True night
flower, midnight-sipped.

Moyra Donaldson

In the Autumn of my Life

Fionn says his friend thinks of Autumn
as being
the most emotionally complex of seasons

and I think – yes –
all that burning beauty in decay
harvested riches of what is past

bright presence of future absence
of what must be endured
before the light comes back

Paula Meehan

Old Biddy Talk

Have you no homes to go to ...

The young mostly on one another's screens
— but these two rapt in each other
at the boundary wall: that genetic imperative,
the force that through the pandemic
drives their flowering, is my spring rain,
is my restorer from the deep-delved wells,
hauled to the healing light of this world
pure water tasting of gemstone & iron,
quartzite & gold:
                   starlight & planets,
the sun & the comets, the moon herself,
she sacred to Brigit, mirrored in my bucket.
My breath, old spirit, stirring in the cowled
reflection of the earth geologic, old seas,
old forests wherein once we swung from tree
to waterlogged tree become shale,
become coal, become diamond.

                       They are fire:
vestal and flame. They are immortal.

from *The Solace of Artemis* (Dublin: Dedalus Press, 2023)

Ivy Bannister

16, 36, 72

1967. I am 16 years old, brimming with ideas, and confident that I know everything. I know, for example, that death is going to sweep me away by the time I am 36. This fact doesn't faze me. I like its bravura, the way it reflects the dazzling workings of my mind... Besides, being 36 is light-years in the future.

Life interests me intensely. For the moment I live in New York City, where nothing is boring. My grandfather, as it happens, is dying in a facility in Queens. Once a week my mother and I take the Q10 bus to visit him. He's in a ward with a half-dozen bed-ridden men, and the place smells awful. The men exist as if they are corpses already, flat on their backs, eyes glazed, bony skeletons scarcely displacing the blankets. It's hard to connect the one who's my relative with the person that I knew and loved: my voluble, excitable grandfather. The nurses come to change his position in bed; and as they lift him, he screams, and I see his bedsores, raw bits of oozing flesh.

By contrast, to die at 36 seems glamorous, dramatic and thrilling – if not downright sensible. Not for me the shrivel of ageing, teeth in the glass, the body of a witch out of the Scottish play, who croaks as she circles a cauldron. Perhaps I'll expire in a fit of 19th century coughing, like Violetta in *La Traviata*, an opera I've just seen that has fired my imagination. Or else, something dark, velvet and feathery will descend from the sky and obliterate me, like an illustration in *The Tales of Edgar Allen Poe*. Whatever the engine of my demise, there will be tears, and I'll be widely mourned; and that's a pleasing thought too.

In the meantime, plans flourish in my head, the ambition to make a mark on the world before my blazing-light exit. For example, I'd like to write an important book; or else, delve into the wonders of the sea: yes, I can picture myself as a scientist at the Marine Biological Laboratory in Woods Hole, Massachusetts. Exactly how I'm going to achieve these things doesn't enter my thinking.

I'm too busy examining the details of the world in my vicinity, which is confined to about a half-mile radius from my home. At school I'm a loner. Good marks come easily, but what really absorbs me is studying my peers. Classes are small, so we sit in a circle of chair desks, facing each other. In spite of our uniforms, there are infinite anomalies to explore. Eyes, hair styles, rings. Socks that stay up, socks that don't. Penny loafers, pencil cases, scents. I can identify the handwriting of every girl in the class. There's a new young maths teacher, whom I adore, but the rest of our teachers are ancients, especially the history teacher. I draw her picture, skewering her eyebags, wrinkles, jowls, and the barnacle growth on her forehead. She is so old.

Around me, the city of New York is in a ferment, but I scarcely notice. Protests against the War in Vietnam and the draft wash over me. When I stumble across a Support Our Boys in Vietnam parade of flag-wavers, I march along for a few blocks, until I get bored. It doesn't cross my mind that other people are not necessarily blessed with lives like mine, a roof over their heads and food on their plates.

1987. Alive and kicking, I've arrived at the age of 36, and death has become the enemy. What an *eejit* I was for imagining that by now, I'd be no more. It feels that my life is still beginning. Unfortunately, I no longer know everything; I wish I did, it would be a great convenience. As the mother of one, with a second on the way, the gaps in my knowledge are only too evident.

I live in Dublin now, and my head is a jumble of changing perspectives. What's happened has not been to plan. The greatest surprise of them all has been the joy of creating life. My babies fill me with wonder. How closely I study them: the perfect limbs and pearly fingernails; the fluff of hair; the silky skin and bright eyes. The lavishness of their beauty astounds me. I can't take my eyes off them, so keen am I to soak in their every detail, before it changes. They learn so fast. 'Dinosaur,' my son yells at his twelve month check-up, pointing to a bright poster. The doctor swivels in amazement, then bursts out laughing.

But there's a dark side to this motherhood business as well: my own self is vanishing. Being on duty 24/7 is a shock; the tiredness is awful. Who knew that every step would feel as if I'm shoving aside the air? Every day is peppered with frustration. Did I really think that I could be a marine biologist? Well, no way is that going to happen now. If only there were time to be me, time to do what I want on my own. Now and again, I snatch moments to write, but the great works of literature that were meant to flow from my pen are not materialising, nothing but staccato scraps of poetry, prose and dialogue. It's impossible not to be jealous of my management consultant husband who gets to read – actually to *read!* – on his grinding weekly air commute between Dublin and Geneva that pays the bills.

Now that I'm a mother, death terrifies me. My romantic view of death is long gone, blown away by the Dublin bombings in 1974. I can still hear the Nassau Street blast, then that nanosecond of shocked silence before the crashing glass. The images of bodies on familiar streets are burnt on my mind. Death is grim, it's ugly and it's everywhere: earthquakes, famine, war, disease.

To keep myself cheerful, I grab a baby and dance around the kitchen, singing along with Tom Lehrer: *We Will All Go Together When We Go*. At all costs, my children must be protected. Single-handedly, I will hold the Grim Reaper at bay. I'll be St. George, I'll be Siegfried. No fire-breathing dragon – nor nuclear warhead – is going to lay waste to me or mine. Death around 36 is for pop stars and rockers, for Jimmy and Janis, for Elvis, even for John Lennon, but not for me.

Fortunately, bit by bit, my life is opening out in new ways. I am no longer a loner. My friends are writers and teachers, artists and actors, mothers like myself. They are women with whom I can talk, bitch, laugh and aspire. We listen to one another, and strive to manage our complicated lives with grace. The objective is to achieve our dreams and build on them in a world that is indifferent to us. I learn about discipline and persistence. *Do, do, do*, I tell myself. My closest friends are all ages. One is her seventies and filled with fun: she's great company, and she inspires me.

Looking in the mirror, I accept what I see, although I douse my wrinkles and crow's feet with moisturiser. If I have grey hairs, there's no time to pluck them. At 36 my fantasies are of survival. With so much to learn and do, why not live forever? And time stretches ahead, infinite and glorious, alive with possibilities.

2023. What, **me**? You're telling me that I'm 72 years old? You've got to be joking. Just how did I get so old so fast?... And whatever you do, do not – repeat, DO NOT – show me the drawings that my 16 year old self would make of me today, skewering my crepy skin, wrinkles and bulging veins.
So. As it happens, I've ignored this ageing thing for years, shoving it to the back of the wardrobe, assuming that the whole disagreeable business has nothing to do with me. I do read a lot of biographies: recently, I've noticed how they all end in the same way. As the poet Robert Herrick put it, '...this same flower that smiles today/ Tomorrow will be dying'.

Surely there must be alternatives? Reincarnation, for example. I'm not fussy, I'll take what I get, preferably something in the vertebrate line: if possible, a songbird, and not a pigeon; or a marine biologist (hah!), and not a mass murderer. Or, please, can I sing like Violetta at the end of *La Traviata*, and pretend-expire only, before I rise from the dead to take my curtain calls?

Protest as I may, the greatest deadline of them all looms ahead, and there's zilch I can do about it. At 72 it seems that I know nothing. Or if I ever knew anything, I've forgotten it.

On the plus side, 72 is not all bad news. To start with, I've gotten this far, which in itself is a gift, my only sibling having died in a plane crash at 51. Luck has favoured me: in education, husband and family; in a wealth of friends on both sides of the Atlantic; in being born after World War II, when advances in medicine have favoured longevity. My ageing body has proved co-operative through thick and thin. I've never taken the bus, not when it's possible to walk; and if my morning exercise routine is uncongenial, the dividends are immediate: my bits still move, mostly fluidly, mostly without complaint.

Best of all, I still love to look at stuff, and there's no end to it – people, plants, animals, buildings, bridges, river, sky – everything, everywhere. Curiosity is my drug of choice, and it floods me with pleasure. I adore absorbing every detail, then hunting out the words to describe what I see in my notebooks. City, countryside, train station: it all fascinates, an ongoing swirl of movement and colour, sound and sensation, nuance and change. Watching a breeze rustling through leafy branches brings me unbridled joy. How mystified I am by people who choose to inhabit their cell-phones, and not the world around them.

A couple of years ago, I found myself in the front row centre of a Broadway theatre waiting to see Glenda Jackson play the title role in Shakespeare's *King Lear*. She was 82 years old, which struck me as – eh – aged. Just how was she going to manage one of the most demanding roles in theatre, a part usually played by a man younger than Lear's supposed fourscore? I needn't have worried. Ms. Jackson surged onto the stage with formidable energy, and swept me up into the hurricane of Lear's emotions. Three hours later, the curtain came down, and I was a limp rag, but Ms. Jackson's bows were brisk. Then it struck me: it was a matinée I'd been watching; and at 8 p.m. Ms. Jackson would be tackling it again, becoming Lear, twice in one day.

'90 is the new 60,' says Muriel Fox, a 95-year-old feminist activist. At 80, didn't Verdi turn towards comedy and life in *Falstaff*? Not to mention Michelangelo and Molly Keane and... Indeed, once you start to look, you find that past and present are alive with productive older people. The imagination persists, and there is always work to be done, the lure of new challenges and new achievements. Nowadays, I thrill to the idea that the best is yet to come.

Máiríde Woods

Things I lost on the way

Things I lost on the way: warm hands,
the morning rattle of Mother
riddling the Rayburn, my father's face
blurred damp on station platforms; desire
childish and overweening for some golden
treasure; phantom poems imagined
but never finished – and hope,
tucked in beside my gawky ambitions.
I could have been someone.

Today a mound of waiting-room advice
flattens my words. Slow decline.
only to be expected. I once dismissed
the wasted faces, hesitant replies
of older relatives, Now, my cold fingers
count the things that remain:
a sliver of beauty, hope cradling truth
and the orange-skin of sorrow.

Tricia Cronin

Letter to my 20-year-old self

Waking up on a glorious sunny May morning I straight away started thinking about what I would say to my 20-year-old self. At 20 my time was my own, as now without family or work responsibilities, but as a student, with reading lists and essay deadlines to shape my days.

My first thought was – Be brave. Or at least go against your instinct to play safe. Don't be afraid to fail, to try something new, to make a fool of yourself. Don't always go for the easy option.

By 20 I'd met the man who turned out to be the love of my life though it took me a few more years to acknowledge that. So I'd say don't be so compliant, be braver, be your more argumentative self, show your true colours early on and fight the battles now rather than years down the line. Don't be so afraid to leave, to travel, to do what he doesn't want to do. Take more risks. Earn the respect you deserve from the start.

And nurture your friendships. You'll need them. A couple of my friends have done that for me through the years when I was too lazy or tired to keep things going. I'm lucky that now in my 60s I still have 3 close friends from school days. When Tess, my best friend, died a few years ago, after a sudden short illness, just as we were both making plans for a busy, active retirement, the 4 of us who'd been at school with her grieved together, closer to her than the family she was estranged from, sharing memories that go back 60 years. Life would have been poorer and more painful without all of them.

Look around your friends now, the students you spend your days and nights with. If you're lucky, or make the effort, some of them could still be part of your life in 50 years time. You'll be surprised who they might be. One of my nurturing friends, a brilliant letter writer, is the common thread that links a group of 18 of us who have reconnected in our later lives and now meet up every year or so. At 20 you can't imagine how good it can feel to look back on shared times and catch up with all the years in between, having spent 3 momentous university years together. I could never have anticipated what a gift that is.

And value those who are old. Talk to your parents, your remaining grandparents and elderly relatives. They won't be around when you realise how much you want to know about their lives and those before them. Ask them questions, mine them for information about the past, listen to their stories. At 20 you take it all for granted: that your grandmother came from a Protetstant family and converted to marry your grandfather, who'd fought with the IRA. When my sister fell pregnant at 20 it came out that my grandmother too had been pregnant before they married. That must've been such a scandal and then a cover-up. Why didn't I ask more questions about them? I knew it had been an unhappy marriage, my mother told me. But there's so much more I don't know. No wonder he couldn't settle on Granma's farm. He wanted to live in America and travelled over and back several times until the Great Depression trapped him in Kerry for good. I remember him as a sad and bitter man, but didn't know why, and in truth wasn't particularly interested. I was a fool then. To my 20-year-old self I'd say, take notice of them, talk to them, listen to their stories. And write them down.

And carry on learning and studying. Carry on writing and painting. Don't give things up because you think you don't have the time or the energy or the talent. Take risks and try harder. I gave up Spanish at 16 because I was too lazy to take the extra classes it meant attending after school. And I gave up chemistry because the teacher warned us it was going to be hard so we'd better leave at the start if we weren't up for the challenge. I stopped writing and drawing because I compared myself to others with more talent or energy and fell far short of my own expectations. I was lazy and didn't want to fail. But do what's hard, what takes time and effort. Learn more languages and work, because it does take work, to become fluent. It means being brave and making the effort. I've watched my son first of all in Spain and now in Italy, throw himself into learning the languages he never studied at school. He talks to everyone and isn't afraid to make mistakes, to be corrected. He takes on challenges and is learning all the time because he has the confidence to fail and keep going. I've tried to learn languages in my 50s and 60s and it's so much tougher than it is at 20. Don't take that ease for granted.

So my final words are the same as my first – Be brave.

But in my arrogance and delusion at 20 I already felt brave. I thought my petty defiance and minor rebellions were courageous. So my words would be wasted. I know I wouldn't have listened.

Jean O'Brien

Praise for Alextrona

As I age winter seems to go on and on
while I long for sunshine's warmth
on skin, and to feel cool seawater
as I gingerly wade in breasting the waves,
to feel luscious sand squelch between
pale toes. I avoid the rocks
with their dark tenants; glissading sea eel,
the nipping crab and darting fish.

As the baptism of sun and briny water works
its miracle of renewal, we feel
whisperings of hope lodge within;
I count my year's losses. Another sibling
gone, taking chunks of childhood with him.
Tears at the graveside as all our losses gather
and sweeten again, as if memory
were a feast to sicken on.

Soon the clocks will move forward,
a small trick we use to let light in.
Summer nights will brighten until
late. New day greets us by slipping
behind the small gaps in the blinds or
curtains and we bow to Alextrona's
urging as light bears everything
away and casts no shadows.
The world and its wide horizons await.

Tricia Cronin

I am amazed

I am amazed sometimes to think how old I am. I can remember the dense London fogs, pea-soupers, before burning coal was banned by the Clean Air Act. That was in 1956 so I must have been 3 or 4, walking to nursery school holding on to the big old-fashioned pram carrying my brother and sister, or clutching my mother's hand.

We lived in Fulham, near a busy street market and a parade of shops. The fog greyed out all colour and muffled the usual morning sounds. The shop lights formed a ghostly haze as we walked along, only able to see a few inches ahead, slowly navigating the narrow, busy pavement with figures looming through the murk around us. I don't remember being frightened but did feel disgust at the black stuff that came out of my nostrils later.

Fulham in the 1950s seemed mostly grey and drab, shabby and grubby and the fogs were part of that. So too was not having a bathroom – I remember going to take a bath in the municipal baths just over the road, where my mum also did the family's washing – later she used the launderette, until she had the luxury of our own twin tub. We had that for many years.

Our house was small and narrow, part of a house we shared with an old lady called Mrs Banyard, with only a tiny, walled back yard, surrounded by high brick walls. So we were often taken to the park, spending hours on end there in the summer, in the playgrounds and greenery of Eel Brook Common or the much bigger Bishops Park which ran alongside the Thames. I loved the special clean smell of the water at high tide. Once we saw the rigging of a small yacht caught in the overhanging trees and some bystanders trying to help untangle it. Why did that sight scare me so much? I didn't want to stay to watch it float free and remember the urgency with which I tried to make my mother move away.

I was disturbed too by the pet shop on a corner we passed on our walk to Bishops Park. Sometimes there was a sad-faced caged monkey in the window. I would try to hurry us past but couldn't help looking at him too and remember how his huge brown eyes followed us.

Jean O'Brien

We Didn't Know Then It Was All A Gift

Only the light moving across the courtyard
marks the time, its movement barely perceptible,
as it touches a chimney here, a window there,
until, when you lift your head from your book,
get up from the desk, lay down your pen
you find it has crossed the yard and is sinking
below the grey slate roofs.

My unruly heart darts back and forth
in it own version of keeping time. It lost
its metronomic fervour some years ago,
it seems to have its own goal in mind and I
have little say. It is just that I feel the need
to catch up with myself, to somehow keep
track of all that glorious passed time.

Lost days spent lying on our backs,
sharing cigarettes and lies,
in barely known rooms with loves
that were so time-consuming and intense
and now only a glimpse of a limb, unexpected bare skin
or a hint of a half remembered colour seen
as if in an ongoing dream helps me keep track.

Spring once sang in us, our young hearts flexible
and strong were given to sudden urgencies.
Winter's song is a low lament, a longing
to turn back and begin again.

Anne Griffin

Change

I've never been afraid of change. Up to turning fifty I pretty much welcomed it. I've changed careers four times and lived in well over ten houses. I change rooms around on whims that come more often than my poor husband might like. That is until recently, when I have begun to doubt myself.

It's a matter of tiredness, I think. Or illness. But mostly age.

Age. It's my recurring theme right now. Ten years ago, at forty-four, I made my biggest career change by becoming a writer. Prior to that I'd been a bookseller, a community development worker and a financial controller in the charity sector. So when I decided to give writing a go, I opened my arms once again and greeted it with joy. For six years thereafter I worked exceptionally hard, working by day, writing by night, raising a family in between. By the time my debut novel, *When All Is Said*, was published in 2019, I had turned fifty and felt I had finally found what I was looking for.

It frightened me too. I'd never been self-employed. Had never wanted to be. I was quite happy for someone else to always worry about the viability of a thing, I simply wanted to do my job well and get paid for it. But here I was now: writer, marketer, financial controller, publicist, all rolled into one. Two things then happened that meant the challenges I'd always been able to rise to suddenly made me doubt those abilities I had so cherished and relied on.

And both came with the ageing process.

I hit the menopause. And I hit it very badly. It had started back when I was forty-eight so you would think that I would have had the measure of it by the time I was fifty. But I hadn't. In fact things went decidedly south. In a year when I was touring with *When All Is Said*, doing every festival there was both in the UK and Ireland and further afield, the symptoms were becoming unbearable. Naturally, I went on HRT, and while, yes, I found that at least I could sleep at night again, I would wake in the morning feeling as if my head had never hit the pillow. By six o'clock in the evening, I'd be asleep on the couch. I started to knit a blanket in order to keep myself awake until nine o'clock, a time I deemed acceptable to finally crawl into bed. Convinced the HRT was causing it, alongside other health issues, I started to come off my patch. On my third visit to my doctor, we finally discovered what was wrong, I was coeliac.

I'm not an expert on coeliac disease. But with the passing of years something had changed within my body that meant I now had an autoimmune condition. Being diagnosed so much later in life had meant it was going to take a lot more time to recover. Nearly two years on from my official diagnosis in 2021, I am beginning to feel better but I'm not sure I'll ever get back to who I was.

My biggest loss due to illness was my absolute faith in myself. I had lost my belief that I could do whatever I liked, once I put my mind to it. Youth, I'd think, perhaps unfairly, brings complete recovery, ageing means something lingers.

I was changing but this time it wasn't my decision.

I became slower to take on anything new. I feared it. I retreated more into myself. I'd think back to the younger me and yearn, in the same way I now longed for a Tayto-crisp batch-loaf sandwich only ten times worse, for the confidence I once had. I'd have traded in that gluten kick for one ounce of what I had before sickness took the legs from under me and made me question myself.

Being one's own boss, and therefore champion, clearly necessitates confidence and an ability to change with society's appetite. A commitment to take on new tasks – teaching creative writing, for example, or writing reviews, screen writing, devising and creating festivals – which at one point in my life would have excited me, now caused untold fear, anxiety and hesitation. In my younger years, I would have swallowed down the doubts, done the research and moved forward. Now, I wondered might I just watch another episode of *Home Rescue*. I was living my life observing others succeed when I was floundering.

I was convinced that things could only get worse. As the years progressed, I was sure my little store of confidence was going to keep lessening if I didn't somehow get off my rear end and try. So I started talking to myself: little things – instructions and mantras.

My first and most effective was: *Just do this one thing*. Instead of trying to juggle too many things, I would choose only one. I started to use this two years back when I was undiagnosed and very ill in order to simply get out of bed, I would say to myself, 'all you need to do is go eat breakfast, that's all I'm asking of you today'. I still use it. So, for example, this week I am doing this one article, nothing else. And once I say this to myself, the rest of my worries about all that is still left to do falls away and I feel unburdened. The beautiful trick here is that once the burden is gone, the fear goes too and quite often by the time the week is out I have achieved much more than that one singular goal.

Then I decided on this: *This is my journey not theirs*. It is far too easy in this world of writing to compare your experience to that of others. I have therefore limited my social media trawling and only use it when I need to put up something about my own work. I stop looking at reviews and the bestseller lists. This is my journey. And my body is telling me to stop looking over the garden fence and tend my own patch. However, there is one exceptional writer I will always keep an eye on: Edna O'Brien, 92 years old, still writing, still brilliant. It is she who demands I stop wallowing.

My next saying, while perhaps not exactly original to the world, it is to me: Say no. I'm learning to distil better. When opportunities come along I weigh them up more and decide if the personal benefit is worth the output. Before, I was forever saying yes, no matter what 'the ask', now I pause and think. I check the wisdom gauge and establish if the energy I have can be put to more beneficial use.

As an introvert this next one takes a bit of getting used to: *Social contact is good*. As well as being tired all the time, I'm very happy to stay away from the world as much as possible. This is not the best of combinations. As I've retreated further onto my couch in the last four years, I've realised I've lost what it is to laugh freely, not sarcastically or begrudgingly, but with the abandon of happiness. I'm finding this one the hardest to follow through on but know that it is key to me regaining the ground that was once mine.

I rarely actually believe this one, but I'm trying: *It's OK to be tired*. Having once been a go getter, I can't seem to come to terms with this slower me. I'm finding it hard to just find my way to accept myself as someone who simply needs to be more mindful of herself.

My last instruction may seem basic but for me it is a necessity: *Eat then move*. If I'm feeling tired, I check two things. Have I eaten? I was always a bad eater, but now I'm pretty hopeless. I would gladly have an intravenous drip rather than having to stop to think about what to eat. With a meal finally consumed, I then ask: Have you done anything other than sit in the chair? That's when I go for a walk or work in the garden or do some activity that will engage my whole body as opposed to just my fingers and mind. It gives me the energy I need to continue.

And in all of this, the biggest challenge is simply accepting that, yes, I am slower and more tired, and nothing I do will totally reverse this but that that is OK. And while I can be wiser in my choices and kinder to myself, the change ahead of me is simply and purely to accept me as I am now, the woman who has achieved and will continue to achieve on a journey that is uniquely and brilliantly her own. I want to stop fearing that I will let myself down based on who I was, and move to a place of admiration of who I am now – the Anne I am becoming as I walk hand in hand with this gift of age.

Lorna Shaughnessy

Crow's Feet

Scraggy-feathered crow against the snow,
rough sketch of winter in charcoal
high stepping on the high wire of survival.

We women of a certain age, crone-crows,
have long outgrown the pretty and reached
the compelling edge, the caw-caustic real.

Moyra Donaldson

I didn't use to hesitate

went out into whatever was coming,
drew it to me, rode into it full tilt.

I used to outrun the shadow
under which I am now waiting.

Catherine Dunne

Invisibility: The New Super Power

Grace and Frankie is a comedy series on Netflix starring Jane Fonda and Lily Tomlin. Fonda and Tomlin play two characters recently abandoned by their husbands of donkeys' years: two middle-aged men who have left their wives to set up home together. Played by Sam Waterston and Martin Sheen respectively, Sol and Robert have been secret lovers for years.

In episode three, Grace and Frankie decide they need cigarettes to help them cope with the recent trauma of their collapsed lives. Grace, Fonda's character, admits she hasn't smoked a cigarette 'since they were good for you'.

The two women stand at the supermarket counter, waiting to be served. But the store clerk ignores them. So they call out to him. He continues to ignore them until, suddenly, success! He makes his way back across the shop floor to the counter, smiling broadly.

'Thank goodness,' says Grace.

But he walks right past her, and instead serves a young blonde woman, who flirts with him and chats about buying lottery tickets. He turns his back on Grace and Frankie, upon which Grace yells at him: 'Are you in a coma?'

He raises one dismissive finger to silence her. He barely glances in her direction. Grace loses it.

She slams a plastic box on the counter, jumps up and down, shrieking 'What kind of animal treats people like this? Can you not see me? Do I not exist?'

Watching Grace 'lose her shit' as Frankie calls it, is funny and Fonda gives it welly. But back in the car, as the women smoke – cigarettes that Frankie stole, while the young man continued not to see her – Grace admits 'That lacked poise'.

Then she hesitates for a second before she says 'But I refuse to be irrelevant.'

Frankie shrugs. 'I learned something,' she says. 'We've got a super power. You can't see me, you can't stop me.'

*

I wonder at what age women begin to become invisible. A quick review of Internet sites suggests that Invisible Women Syndrome usually hits at around fifty. While *Grace and Frankie* touches on the comical moments, there is a darker, more disturbing side to this invisibility.

In her 2019 book, *Invisible Women*, Caroline Criado Perez exposes the world's design faults: faults that have far greater impact on women's lives than our being ignored in shops, or pushed past in queues. She dedicates her book to 'the women who persist: keep on being bloody difficult'[1]. *Invisible Women* explores the power of the 'default male' – the startling reality that everything in our daily lives has been built around men: from keyboards and mobile phones at one end, to 'stab vests and car crashes', and even snow-clearing, at the other. The world is not designed for women.

Criado Perez quotes Simone de Beauvoir at the beginning of her book, who says: 'Representation of the world, like the world itself, is the work of men; they describe it from their own point of view, which they confuse with absolute truth'.

And lest you think Criado Perez presents a radically divergent point of view just for the sake of it, or her own completely off-the-wall version of truth, *Invisible Women* won the Science Book Prize of the Royal Society in 2019.

Incidentally, she also campaigned successfully to have Jane Austen's face on a UK banknote, two hundred years after the author's death. V.S. Naipaul criticised Austen's work as 'narrow', Criado Perez says, vividly recalling Virginia Woolf's statement in 1929 that a critic deems a book to be 'insignificant' because 'it deals with the feelings of women in a drawing room'. However, 'a book that deals with war' is automatically an 'important book'.

It's a critical response, she suggests, that is not unfamiliar to women writers today.

*

So how do we counter the spectre of invisibility as we age?

Statista.com, in a survey released in May 2023, shows that in 2021, the average life expectancy for women in Ireland was 84.1 years. That implies the possibility of more than three decades after the watershed birthday of fifty – if we're very lucky – all filled to the brim with the potential to 'persist', to keep on being – or even beginning to be – 'bloody difficult'.

In her 1970 book, *La vieillesse*, published in England as *Old Age*, but interestingly, in the United States as *The Coming of Age*, de Beauvoir declares:

> 'There is only one solution if old age is not to be an absurd parody of our former life, and that is to go on pursuing ends that give our existence a meaning — devotion to individuals, to groups or to causes, social, political, intellectual or creative

[1] Caroline Criado Perez, *Invisible Women* (Penguin Random House, 2019).

work... In old age we should wish still to have passions strong enough to prevent us turning in on ourselves. One's life has value so long as one attributes value to the life of others, by means of love, friendship, indignation, compassion'.[2]

Such ageing seems to me to be the polar opposite of invisibility: even if the only person to whom we become visible is, in the end, ourselves. Devotion to family and friends, or to a cause; compassion for others' suffering, even indignation: these are not necessarily virtues on public display, but no matter how quietly we espouse them, they can become our own shining lights of meaning and purpose.

*

This, of course, assumes that we are not trapped somewhere on, or below, the poverty line; that we are able to live with dignity and freedom; that we are not ground down by the relentless duties of caring. Recent studies suggest that four factors are essential to 'successful' ageing: physical health, psychological health, social support and leisure activity.

Being a full-time carer, particularly an ageing one, exerts pressure on all four factors.

According to a recent study conducted by Trinity College Dublin: 'In Ireland, there are approximately 500,000 family carers who play a vital role in supporting people with additional needs, physical or intellectual disabilities, frail older people, those with palliative care needs or those living with chronic illnesses, mental health challenges or addiction'.[3]

Recently, on a radio chat show, I heard the word 'carer'. I turned up the volume.

It is a phone-in. Carers all over the country call to describe their days. Mothers and fathers with life-limited children. Men and women with partners suffering from dementia.

Adult children with parents who go missing, sneaking out of the house in the small hours, wandering off into the traffic; taken back home to safety again and again. Caller after caller speaks of feeling abandoned. Of a Health Service that continually lets them down. Of a system that dehumanises the people they love, strips them of their dignity, makes them beg for what every citizen should be able to claim as their right.

[2] Simone de Beauvoir, *Old Age* (Harper Collins, 1972).
[3] Professor Dominic Trépel, TCD School of Medicine, *The Value of Unpaid Care in Ireland, and how economic consequence varies by social, economic and health condition* (2023).

But there are other stories, too. Stories of devotion and sacrifice; stories of love undiminished. Stories of ingenuity and resilience.

You're all saints, the presenter says. Anyone who cares in this way is a saint.

I've heard this before. Those exact words, or other wide-eyed variations. And all of them set my teeth on edge.

Saints don't need practical support: they already have God's ear and some supernatural powers of their own. Saints don't need a break from their saintliness. Saints can be revered, cherished, even beseeched. And they ask nothing of us, other than our devotion.

Carers on the other hand, work themselves to a standstill. They save the state a fortune.

Without them, the whole creaking edifice of our 'Health Service' – itself neither healthy nor a service for those who most need it – would collapse, falling in on itself like trees felled in the forest.

This is the aspect of ageing in Ireland that most frightens me. The prospect is terrifying: that I might become a burden to those I love. Such fear fuels my motivation to stay as healthy as I can, emotionally and physically; as socially engaged as I can, able to balance work and leisure as carefully as I can.

*

I feel fortunate to have my own creative work, and even more fortunate to have a precious network of family, friends and colleagues who intersect with that work. The existence of such a community of shared values contains within it the necessity of looking beyond the self to the wider world of people of courage: towards those brave men and women who place their lives on the line as they persist in speaking truth to power. Persist, indeed, in 'being bloody difficult'.

Simone de Beauvoir's insistence in on the need to 'attribute value to the life of others, by means of love, friendship, indignation, compassion' is one that resonates strongly with me. Working within Irish PEN/PEN na hÉireann, speaking into the silence of those whose voices have been suppressed or cancelled, means that I have come face to face with the courage of poets and journalists and novelists everywhere.

Above all, I came to know the quiet, persistent, steely courage of Victoria Amelina, an exceptional human being and an outstanding writer. A tireless activist, Victoria documented Russian war crimes in Ukraine, giving voice to the grief of the voiceless.

On the first of July 2023, Victoria died as a result of a Russian missile strike on a pizza restaurant in Kramatorsk. She was thirty-seven years of age, mother to a twelve-year-old son.

Hilary Mantel, in an interview with *The Paris Review*, said: 'The question is not who influences you, but which people give you courage'.[4] Victoria is one of those people.

*

It would be impossible to face the reality of ageing without accepting the inevitability of loss. It's unlikely that any of us will reach a ripe old age – whatever that is – without having lost loved ones. Grief is the price we pay for love, and it is a painful, all consuming one.

Several years ago, I wrote a personal essay for *The Death of a Child*.[5] In the writing, I raged against the notion that grief has its tidy stages, that we move neatly from denial to anger to bargaining to acceptance. That we can fix our grief and find closure. I hated that word then: and I hate it still.

Years later, it was a relief to come across this paragraph in *The Examined Life* by Stephen Grosz. He writes: 'My experience is that closure is an extraordinarily compelling fantasy of mourning. It is the fiction that we can love, lose, suffer and then *do something* to permanently end our sorrow. We want to believe we can reach closure because grief can surprise and disorder us – even years after our loss'.[6]

I do not want to suggest that grief is a necessary paralysis to which we have to succumb for ever: on the contrary, we must find ways to navigate our way through it – but like raising a child, grief takes a village.

Over the years, I have come to rely on my community of 'grief eaters'. The phrase is a translation from the Urdu: 'ghum-khaur' – the people who gather together to consume the mourner's sorrow. 'There are no words in that language for a solitary grieving; no concept of the privacy of loss. No-one is ever left to mourn alone. Instead, family, friends, members of the community, all protect the bereaved one, closing in, devouring their grief for them so that the burden might be lightened'.

*

I opened this essay with a scene from *Grace and Frankie*. I will now close it with a scene from *Fried Green Tomatoes at the Whistle Stop Café*. I do so in the spirit of celebrating a freedom that, if we're very lucky – that word again:

[4] Hilary Mantel, *The Art of Fiction, Paris Review*, Issue 226 (Spring 2015).

[5] Catherine Dunne, "Eoin", *The Death of a Child*, ed. Peter Stanford (London: Continuum, 2011).

[6] Stephen Grosz, *The Examined Life* (London: Vintage, 2013).

perhaps 'privileged' is more accurate – comes with advancing age. Evelyn Couch, played by Kathy Bates, encounters two skimpily-clad young women who 'steal' the parking space she had her eye on. They laugh, and say 'Face it, lady, we're younger and faster'.

Evelyn accelerates and smashes into their car, while they look on in horror.

'What are you doing?' they cry. 'Are you crazy?'

Evelyn smiles. 'Face it, girls,' she says. 'I'm older and I have more insurance'.

Kerry Hardie

The New Dead

Our bodies come from the earth, they belong to the earth,
yearn to lie down in the earth and rest, to look up

at the black light over the valley, everything staged
for a world we no longer inhabit.

Ours is the wonder of non-being, passing beyond –
our flesh of no more concern

than a daisy picked by a child and let fall,
or a rabbit, after the jacketing knife,

has slid down its belly,
unpeeled the warm coat,

leaving entrails and bones
muddling the blood-grained deal table.

from *We Go On* (Bloodaxe Books, 2024)

Meadhbh Ní Bhrádaigh

'If you didn't know what age you were, what age would you say you were?'

That's the slogan that came out many years ago for a dedicated 'Year of Older People'.

I put it on my desk. It emblazoned itself in my brain.

For me it begs the question, and answers it – that at different times, with different events and with different people, I can be *all manner of ages.*

In late **Spring and the Summer** I am brimming with energy – digging the garden, foraging in the forest for wild garlic, thrilled to accept the offer of a boat ride on the local lake, eager to walk the open road to hear the gushing thrill of the cuckoo. I am a child again following her tantalising warble, as she glides elusively from tree to tree.

Last year, seeing the brown earth of the flat bog-land in the midlands, I yearned to run across the peat in my bare feet. I was out of sight of the world. It was the earthiest of experiences bottled in my senses, for revisiting on later grey and rainy days.

Summer calls for bright colours and sling-back shoes. It's the season when young and old can act the peacock and strut their stuff. It's a time for paradoxes and silliness, a time for pink and yellow and all sorts of mismatch. For me, to think and act middle-aged is more an invitation than a challenge. To dare to climb a mountain and cycle the Greenway (in the exhilarating company of junior family members) is high on 'the bucket list'. The time as Jenny Joseph says, in her poem 'Warning', 'when people who know me are not too shocked or surprised'.[1]

It is my time too, for peering into the hot press and attacking a few hefty washes of bedlinen, woollen jumpers, towels, clothing, anything that can be washed and hung out for days on end to 'freshen them up', as my mother would say.

As **Autumn** rolls on I become aware of the falling leaf, and the pervading mellowness. I am more subdued. Visits to the library increase, the summer gear is shelved, lavender balls put between the layers of all that is stacked away. I return to the garden, a little sadder and with less gusto to empty the

---

[1] Jenny Joseph, "Warning". 1961.https://www.scottishpoetrylibrary.org.uk/poem/warning/

pots and de-head the roses. The shortening days invite longer indoor time with family, friends, housebound.

How am I in Winter? As I grow into older age, Winter invades my psyche more acutely. It is a time of warm escape from the fast lane, a time of blazing fires, contemplation, books, crosswords, a shot at penning a few lines, and unashamed idleness. A time when the deep glow of friendship envelopes us to share and ponder our yesteryears and hopefully energise one another for tomorrow. In the northern hemisphere, the Feast of Christmas illuminates the darkness.

Hygge, as the Scandinavians call it, is the time to cosy up, light the candles and give oneself permission to slow down.... the ideal season to be in tune with, and grateful for the mysteries of nature. The squirrels, moles, bees and hedgehogs hibernate, the birds more or less silence their song, and the trees become de-nuded of their leaves. On the human side, the wintry season teases us, and sometimes makes an exhibition of our jerky arthritic limbs. That said, I am older than my mother ever was and for that I am grateful.

I applaud the great Thomas Merton who had a strong love and insight into the seasons, when he says **'I can only desire this absurd business of the trees that say nothing. I am happy as a coot...and I cannot explain it'**.[2]

---

[2] Thomas Merton. *When the Trees Say Nothing: Writings on Nature.* Sorin Books, 2003.

Lorna Shaughnessy

Pollarding

Let me age like a pollarded oak
Let my cropped crown make space for pliant branches

Let my stunted height protect me from windblow
Let me become small and wizened without losing my sap

Let my skin gnarl into scars for every cut,
my chin, nose and ears sprout epicormic whiskers

Let me be   hollowed out
Let holly   flourish
      inside me,
hugging and strangling
      till I become
part holly
          part oak.

Let my empty trunk be home to all the
c r e e p i n g and c r a w l i n g
creatures of the woods.

Let me be home to mosses, lichens and ferns
and all my new limbs grow up and out
                            away from me.

Heather Ingman

Memory and Ageing[1]

Why, as we age, do we remember some things and not others? This is the question Virginia Woolf poses at the start of her memoir, 'A Sketch of the Past':

> Why have I forgotten so many things that must have been, one would have thought, more memorable than what I do remember? Why remember the hum of bees in the garden going down to the beach, and forget completely being thrown naked by father into the sea? (Mrs Swanwick says she saw that happen).[2]

As I approach my seventies, I sometimes think that memories are my richest possession, yet until recently I found it difficult, such was the distance I had travelled from the places of my childhood, to tap into them.

One hot day last summer I was sitting in the gardens of Trinity College, Cambridge, the very college that refused Woolf access to its library on account of being a woman, trying to catch my breath. I was recovering from a bout of Covid which had left me listless and lethargic. As I drowsed in front of the sweet-smelling wildflower meadow that has replaced the college lawns on which Woolf was forbidden to tread, I was thinking about a book I had recently purchased. Celia Paul's series of fictional letters to Gwen John, an artist with whom she feels a particular affinity.[3] I was wondering whether, after a long career of teaching women's writing in Dublin, there was any writer to whom I would feel close enough to address in a series of letters. I remembered the Irish writer, Elizabeth Bowen, born in Dublin in 1899, and as I thought about her, I began to see that parts of her life overlapped with mine. Not literally – I was twenty when she died – but the more I thought about it the more I discovered similarities. As I went on thinking about Bowen over the following weeks and months, I found that reflecting on her life was giving me the key to my own.

---

[1] With the kind permission of the publisher, some material in this chapter has been reproduced from Heather Ingman, *A Modern Literary Life. Elizabeth Bowen*, a memoir published by EER in 2023.

[2] Virginia Woolf, *Moments of Being*, ed. Jeanne Schulkind (New York: Harvester, 1985), 70.

[3] Celia Paul, *Letters to Gwen John* (London: Jonathan Cape, 2022).

On the face of it, it would seem unlikely that someone from the North of England would have anything in common with an Anglo-Irish writer born five decades earlier, a class, almost 'a race', as Bowen herself would have said, apart. I first came to her work in my early thirties when I had already been living in Ireland for several years. I found her conservative views off-putting and the irregularities of her style, famously compared by Woolf to trying to throw a lasso with a knotted rope, exasperating. Yet in her essay, 'Out of a Book', Bowen speaks of 'the overlapping and haunting of life by fiction' for anyone who 'reads deeply, ravenously, unthinkingly, sensuously, as a child'.[4] We recognise ourselves, remake ourselves and remember ourselves through reading, she suggests. This was what was happening to me. Reading and rereading Elizabeth Bowen, one of the greatest twentieth-century writers to come out of Ireland, was helping me remember my life.

As I pictured Bowen, in her late fifties, driving away for the last time from Bowen's Court, the Big House that had been in the Bowen family since 1775, my memories of Knockdrin Castle outside Mullingar owned since 1961 by my parents-in-law, Hans and Irene von Prondzynski, came spilling out. I remembered the terraced lawns where our sons played football, the walled garden where Irene was to be found working most afternoons, and the woods where we used to walk. Two of the original Anglo-Irish owners of Knockdrin, the Levinges, are buried here, Godfrey who was refused burial in the churchyard because he took his own life, and beside him, Henry, who chose to be buried in the woods and not in consecrated ground, out of loyalty to his brother. I remembered all the people over the years who had worked on the farm, especially Michael and his family who lived in the house across the courtyard. A slight man, Michael was a huge presence in Knockdrin. He knew where all the wires went, where the taps were, how the pipes worked. He taught our elder son to ride a bike when I had despaired. Years after his death, whenever we drew up in the courtyard, I looked across for Michael to step out of his house and welcome us.

It has been over three years since the castle was sold. We all still remember the scraping noise the back door made on the tiles, the dull thud of the swing doors leading into the kitchen and the early morning sound of Irene opening the heavy wooden shutters in the schoolroom, the yellow sitting room, the ballroom, and the library. We all remember the uneven stone steps on the terraced lawns that once led down to a tennis court and a rose

[4] *The Mulberry Tree: Writings of Elizabeth Bowen* edited by Hermione Lee (London: Vintage, 1999), 48.

garden, and the sound of the cows on the dairy walk plodding back to the dairy to be milked. We remember the swifts that returned each year, the bats that swooped and dived on summer nights and, as Bowen puts it, were 'a trouble to many'.[5] We remember the purple aubretia that flowered every spring along the garden wall, the sweet taste of Irene's grapes in the glasshouse and her white raspberries in the walled garden. In the house where we now live, we are surrounded by memories of Hans and Irene, in the portraits of Hans' ancestors hanging on the walls, and in the many views of Knockdrin painted over the years by different hands. These bitter-sweet memories, of love and loss, enrich our lives in old age.

Reading Bowen's descriptions of her schooldays at Lindum, Harpenden Hall and Downe House, I smell the rusty ink in the inkpots and hear the scratching of our pen nibs across the paper and I marvel that girls' education had changed so little in the fifty years since Bowen was at school that I am able to draw comparisons with my own schooldays in the 1960s. Like Dinah and her gang of three in Bowen's novel, *The Little Girls* (1964), I was part of a band of four girls. We sat together in class, walked home together after school, pausing greedily at the sweet shop, and were in and out of one another's houses in the holidays. Like Dinah and her friends we differed sharply in temperament and interests yet because we spent our daily lives in each other's company for so many years I still have the, no doubt erroneous, impression whenever we meet up, as we do from time to time, that I can predict at any given moment how they will react, in a way I am unable to with more recent friends. No matter what we have gone through over the years, something of our essential selves, formed during those bedrock school years, endures. As Bowen, that acute observer of schoolgirls, noted, 'Such young friendships, first friendships, are indissociable from our own identities; they colour life for us, and the colour stays'.[6] This has been one of my discoveries as I age.

As a young girl, Bowen listened to her mother and aunts talk so often about France, that it came to seem for her magical: 'I had heard so much about France, it appeared too good to be true – might it not, after all, be a sort of fairy-tale land?'[7] Reading this unlocked another memory. I recalled how, growing up in the 1960s, my friends and I thought France was pretty

[5] Elizabeth Bowen, *Bowen's Court and Seven Winters* (London: Virago, 1984), 28.

[6] *People, Places and Things: Essays by Elizabeth Bowen* edited by Allan Hepburn (Edinburgh: Edinburgh University Press, 2008), 139.

[7] *The Weight of a World of Feeling. Reviews and Essays by Elizabeth Bowen* edited Allan Hepburn (Evanston: Northwestern University Press, 2017), 162-3.

much the ideal place to live. We absorbed French music (Johnnie Halliday, Jacques Brel, France Gall), spoke scraps of French to each other during break times, debated the merits of Camus versus Sartre. We wanted to visit the Café de Flore and sit at the feet of Jean-Paul Sartre and Simone de Beauvoir. We wanted to wear black polo necks, smoke Gauloises, and drink lots of black coffee. We wanted to look like Jane Birkin.

My cousins grew up in that impossibly glamorous country across the Channel in Ville-d'Avray, a mere seven miles from the centre of Paris. Thanks to them, I visited France and encountered Paris before I knew London or Dublin. I was eight years old, the same age as Jeremy in *Eva Trout* (1968), and like him I was dazzled by the buildings and amazed by 'the wide-open extravagance of the Right Bank perspectives and spaces'.[8] As the narrator says of Jeremy, so it might have been said of me that I had never before, or even perhaps since, seen so much of anything as I saw of Paris on that visit. Inspired by that visit I later spent a summer in France as au pair and a year teaching English in Grenoble. For ten years, I lectured in French at Trinity College, Dublin and spent my vacations rummaging through Paris libraries. Though events later took me down a different path, reading Bowen's francophile essays and novels brought back those years when journeying between Ireland and France played such an important part in my life.

Mental illness and disability ran through Bowen's family life, as it has through my own. Reading Bowen's account of her father's breakdown, later transposed into her portrayal of Emmeline in *To the North* (1932), brought back memories of my much loved grandmother who fought bipolar disease all her life. Bowen grew up, as I did, watchful for mental illness in loved ones. Accounts of Bowen's lifelong struggle with her pronounced stammer, and her portrayal of Jeremy's difficulties with language in *Eva Trout*, unspooled memories which I had suppressed for years of my own childhood lisp and the endless elocution classes, much resented at the time, which saved my career as a lecturer.

Ageing and retirement have granted me leisure to look at Bowen in a different light from the years when I was constrained by teaching to a syllabus. My appreciation of Bowen has altered with the different stages of my life. When I was younger, it was Bowen's sharp, often coruscating, dialogue that appealed to me. Now I look beneath the surface for what is not being said in her novels, for uneasy fractures, silences, and ellipses in the conversations. When I was younger, I was absorbed by Bowen's descriptions

---

[8] Elizabeth Bowen, *Eva Trout, or Changing Scenes* (London: Vintage, 1999), 204.

of young women trying to find a place for themselves in a society where the text for their lives was seemingly determined from the outset. When I became a mother, I read her for her portrayal of women's often ambivalent feelings towards motherhood and for her perceptive and always moving portraits of children. Nowadays I find myself most drawn to her presentations of ageing women, Antonia in *A World of Love* (1955) and Dinah, Sheila, and Clare in *The Little Girls*, coping with life's setbacks as best they can. I take a closer look at the black and white photographs of Bowen in late middle age, admiring her attention to detail, the well-cut tweed suits enhanced by carefully chosen scarves, flamboyant brooches, showy earrings, and ropes of pearls. This is a woman who knows how to dress as she ages. What a long way she has travelled from her wedding day and that disastrously shapeless frock with the uneven hem. One advantage of ageing is that we learn, painfully, what suits us and what doesn't.

Like all great writers, Bowen inspires her readers to become not merely readers of her work but, in Proust's words, readers of their own lives:

> Every reader is, while she is reading, the reader of her own self. The writer's work is merely a kind of optical instrument which she offers to the reader to enable her to discern what, without this book, she would perhaps never have perceived in herself. [9]

Gazing on Bowen's landscapes and characters has unlocked, in old age, memories of the people and places that have come to be the story of my life.

---

[9] Marcel Proust, *In Search of Lost Time, Volume VI: Time Regained* translated by Andreas Mayor and Terence Kilmartin, revised by D. J. Enright (London: Vintage, 2000), 273. In a move which Proust, who earlier in this paragraph has invited 'inverts' to give his heroines a masculine countenance, may not have disapproved of, though Bowen certainly would, I have altered Proust's pronouns.

Nessa O'Mahony

Rampike on Montpelier Hill

Nature has done its worst,
be it lightning strike or gale
or air-born virus browning leaves,
drying bark to skeletal.
The whine of saw on wind
is only the latest threat.

Grey sentinel of the slope,
your silhouette encourages
our leaden first steps
before we forget the effort
and limbs acclimatise, thin air
charged with birdsong.

Negative of its former self,
erect still, though no sap courses,
no buds form on desiccated twigs.
Woodpecker's hollow tap
persists, drilling faith
in new life.

Years have passed,
and still it stands,
reminding us
to put one foot
in front of another,
on the ascent or descent.

Mary Dorcey

The Breath of History

'Going down the stairs now

Behind your contrary, infant steps
I want to pick you up
and carry you
or launch you down the bannister
as you did me in this house
Where we played, making up

Childhood together. But time
has come round or run out -
now you must take every step
first along this passage way,
we daughters follow after, each
one of us moving into the space

Cleared by our Mothers'.

(from 'Moving Into the Space Cleared By Our Mothers,' Salmon Poetry, 1991)

These mornings, especially if it is a cold one, as I go down stairs behind my own, now painful steps, I recall this poem and I laugh aloud. How can words written thirty years ago or more, when I was young, passionate and careless, have come round so soon to find me out!

Did I think it would never happen to me? How could I be taken by surprise?

So how do I feel now about getting older than I have been? Much of what I have published so far on the subject has been about my mother who died at ninety-two. I see now that it was possible to be calm, even lyrical on the subject very often because then I was writing about a parent who was forty years ahead of me. By turns jaunty or stoic, she cast a veil of gentle self-mockery over the indignities and theatrical trappings of age. Her unusual courage and her particular brand of abiding faith gave me a foothold against the flood.

Do we not we all desire if we have a good life, more years to enjoy it? And the challenge of ageing is that we very have little say in the matter. We discover that our only true power is to live in the moment, for the moment.

After my mother's death I faced new challenges. But I was surprised to discover that following a break of a year or so, my writing began to flow more strongly than ever and many benevolent and creative new influences entered my life. I have always counted myself fortunate in many ways. And still do. Apart from the osteo knees and fingers that ache from too much typing, I feel fit and well and mentally energetic. I have the rare blessing of chosen work, steady purpose and loving companionship. I've had more than my share of adventure, wonderful and inspiring friendships, more than my fair share of love and romance and of course a lifelong passion for literature, music, activism and friendship. Delight in the company of soul mates.

What more can any of us ask for?

> 'I want to be walking down an avenue in summer, my arm
> about my beloved. I want the avenue tree-lined, my hand
> about your waist, the boughs above our heads arched,
> the brindled light throwing open the path before us...'

(Summer, 2012)

I still love walking down an avenue in summer, my arm around my beloved as this earlier poem recounts. I want my one and only beloved, and many more avenues.

In many ways an adventurer and romantic, when I bring to the fore my memories of childhood I see that it was both challenging and enchanted. We lived on the very lap of the Irish Sea, beside what was then a working fishing harbour. The great hungry beast thrashed loudly, night after night in the harbour below my cot. Listening to all the sounds of the sea, I learned to love adventure, risk taking and the thrilling beauty of the natural world. I had stories and song, swimming and rowing, love and adventure.

My father hurried home every evening to be with us. I waited at the window to catch the first glimpse. And as soon as our tea was finished we three youngest gathered round the fire while he read a different story for each of us. And on summer evenings, he took us out rowing.

But even enchanted years can contain great sorrows. In our case our little haven was blown apart by my father's third and final heart attack when I was seven years of age. I had never seen my mother in tears before the day of his death. And though she always turned her face away, how often did I see it afterwards?

Explaining to adults how my father had died, as one always had to do in that era, I was aware of a strange irony when I told them that he had been an actuary: a profession dedicated to estimating and quantifying risk!

But his premature death taught me to take nothing in life for granted and to concentrate on the now. This early lesson has proved to be a blessing. It may keep my eye on the central questions and my head above the water.

Remembering this, I wonder if it was also the first spark of what became my passion for social justice and human rights? Did I learn my first lesson about injustice and unearned hardship from our straightened circumstances (as people put it then) after my father's death? Because even life in what was considered a wealthy area showed me huge inequalities all around. This was increased by the experience of living in a 'one parent household'. 'What does your father do for a living?' the most often question asked of of a child in the fifties. When I told them he was dead they immediately regarded me with pity. 'Oh god love your poor mother, how will she ever manage'. So I learned to dodge this by telling them she was a 'highly placed harpist!'

I was also deeply influenced by the courage my mother showed, though often stressed to her limit she managed with grace and gallantry. A civil servant for ten years before her marriage she found that just as a married woman was not allowed to remain in the service, neither could a widow return to it (sic). The stain of accomplished heterosexuality was apparently too noxious to allow the sinner to mingle with the chaste.

And could this have been my first experience of gender inequality?

> 'I am not an ordinary woman.
> I wake in the morning
> I have food to eat,
> No one has come in the night
> to steal my child, my lover
> I live where I want,
> I sleep when I'm tired
> I write the words I think
> I can watch the sky
> and hear the sea.
> I am not an ordinary woman'.

Copyright Mary Dorcey, 1991

I wrote this in 1991. And though there was as usual great oppression and injustice in the world, the skies overhead were clear and rose-tinted compared with today.

In February 2021, I was immensely pleased and happy to launch my tenth book *Life Holds its Breath* (Salmon Poetry). But how could I have foreseen that on the very day of its launch Russian bombs would rain down on the sleeping head of children in Ukraine? This ongoing tragedy has darkened and scarred all our days since.

Yet even more menacing clouds have appeared over our heads as I write these words.

Our politicians and technocrats are gathering across the 'free world' this very week, Artificial Intelligence they tell us, is already one step ahead of most human brains and gaining pace every hour. Those who know, who built the things, say it may no longer be possible to impede the rise of this new species on our earth, neither by legislation or improved science. I wish I could believe this was exaggeration.

Along with this existential threat, we have also the warning of global famine, international warfare on a scale we have not seen before and pollution of our skies and seas.

So how do I feel about ageing in this climate? It is not a cheerful prospect. Who could want to face it? But if I must, I hope for as long as possible to remain a woman with an unusual life. I want to guard the capacity to join in collective action and to stand against the tide with comrades.

I divert myself with familiar pleasures: reading, writing, walking, and beloved companionship. I still have wanderlust, as of old. I have lived in six countries and travelled across the world. I've always been inspired by curiosity about people and cultures. When I am stuck for something entertaining to do on sleepless nights, instead of counting sheep, I count the places I've lived.

An activist since I was a schoolgirl, this gave way very early to the fascination with international politics and political theory. I marched in protest with my elder brother to the American Embassy in Dublin during the Vietnam war and accompanied him on Anti-Apartheid marches a few years later. This led to my going to live with my French boyfriend in Paris to study politics and sociology where I very quickly got involved in student politics.

Back in Dublin when I was twenty-two, I got together with six other newly formed activists and established the first Gay Rights Group in Ireland: 'The Sexual Liberation Movement'.

But by far the greatest adventure in those early years was, after several happy relationships with men friends, to meet a French woman at the first gay disco we organised in Dublin, and fall at once deeply in love. This relationship changed my life.

I am immensely proud of all that we in the Gay Community have achieved in the fifty years since our first UCD conference where I was barraged from the floor, abused and threatened because in my speech I dared to proclaim myself a woman who loved women. I am equally proud of what we Women's Liberationists have achieved in Ireland since the nineteen seventies.

When I consider the question of how best to negotiate the years ahead I look to the example of all the courageous women in history including so many from my own country and especially our great women writers who I read and reread: Elisabeth Bowen, Molly Keane, Edna O'Brien and Eavan Boland, to name only four, though we have more than any country should expect.

I live in a beautiful place surrounded by natural beauty. My greatest pleasures are walking and listening, writing, reading, spending lazy, delighting days with my beloved life partner.

> 'Youth come again and
> summer, honeyed light,
> fragrant ground,
> everything new, as of old,
> starting out wide-eyed
> the self yields once more
> to story, a novel thrown open,
> leaves uncut'.

Copyright Mary Dorcey, 2022

There are many things I still want to do and many I want to repeat. I have a book of memoirs to finish and a new collection of novellas in progress. There are friends I want to visit and countries I would like to see again or for a first time. Can I justify the pollution caused by flying?

This June I have been honoured by the invitation to act as the Grand Marshall for the Dublin Gay Pride March in Dublin. It is fifty years since our small group, women and men, met in that upstairs room in Trinity College and founded that first Gay Liberation Group in Ireland. I can think of no better way of celebrating growing older than I have been before.

I will take delight in confounding, for as long as possible, the conventional expectation of ageing gracefully. And to march through the streets of my city, surrounded by thousands of women and men of all ages and varieties, to celebrate this one great battle won for human justice, and proclaim our triumph in being together: free and proud, loving the ones we choose to love.

Mary Rafferty

What I don't need

I don't need scarves, neither those of garish colours nor those carefully chosen for grey hair and older skin.

Hand cream
Candles or scented room diffusers.
Tiny cacti in novelty planters.
Artwork created by small children.
Photographs, no matter how cute, even of those I love.
Beautiful ceramic bowls.
Another vase.
The must-have spice, flavouring or food, even if it's artisan, local or limited edition.
A cookery book.
A recipe.
Any summary of someone else's life lessons.

Any do-dah to put on any surface, no matter what it's made of, where it's made or what mystical, transformative or liberating process is involved.

Anything with a strapline, logo or inspiring message making reference to my one wild and precious life.

Chocolate made on an island that can only be accessed twice a year, using beans that grow inside out, with salt mined from prehistoric landfills.

An app.
Advice on decluttering.
A book on Swedish death-cleaning.
Earrings or any jewellery.
Assumptions about my views, beliefs, experience.

Recommendations for tv programmes, podcasts, restaurants, sights or experiences.

What I need

Smiles
Laughter
Good jokes
Time
Interesting and challenging ideas
Hard questions
Music
Art
Poetry – good poetry, written with skill and care
Walks on city streets, in urban parks, on beaches, on gentle hills
Long, wandery lunches
City breaks
Beauty
Things to make and hold, to give away
To be asked
To be held in mind

To be stretched and used

Wonder at the mundane and everyday
Unfinished business

Arja Kajermo

Recovery Room

She woke up. It was dark.

She could hear somebody breathing. Maybe more than one person. There was a burning feeling in her stomach. Her mouth was dry. Her throat was sore.

There was a subdued light from the open door to her right. Somebody was out there and moving nearer.

A girl dressed in a white tunic and trousers came in with a rattling metal tray. She stopped at the bed across. A doe-eyed girl with a baldy head sat up. There was a whispered conversation.

She could hear the word 'pain' said many times. The nurse held up an injection needle and mumbled that soon there would be no pain. The girl sank into the pillows.

The nurse came over to her. 'Are you in pain?' Was she in pain? 'I thought I was in the recovery room?' she said.

'You are in the oncology ward, dearie', the nurse whispered. 'You've had major surgery. Do you want something for pain?'

Oncology ward? Major surgery? No, that wasn't her! An appendix isn't major. It's keyhole surgery. The nurse was probably overworked on her night shift and had got her patients mixed up. She said she was not in pain. When the nurse walked away she regretted it. Always say yes to pain relief when it is offered. Hoard it for later when pain finds you down the line. The nurse moved on to the next bed. Everyone said they were in pain. Same question. Same answer.

She tried to remember yesterday. When was yesterday? Was it when her GP sent her in to A & E with suspected appendicitis? Yes, that was yesterday. That sorted in her head, she dozed off, drifting slowly up towards the ceiling like vapour. She saw the beds and the people lying in them from above. Then she felt herself falling suddenly and landing with a thud on the bed! What the...! Her heart was racing with the fright of it. She was drenched in sweat. Should she ring the bell and get the nurse? She rang the bell.

The nurse came and whispered 'Are you in pain?' She wanted to say that she had just fallen from a great height. 'I am unwell', she said instead, 'I am hot.' The nurse said she would get the doctor. The nurse came back with a boy doctor who was rubbing his eyes like a child just lifted out of bed. He asked how she felt. She said 'I'm very unwell!' He looked dubious. 'I'm hot', she persisted, 'Hot!' The doctor said 'Yes, it's quite hot in here, dear.' Did he think he had been invited to discuss the ambiance of the room? Dear? Old dear? He patted her arm. They left.

The next time she woke daylight flooded the room. The trolleys from the canteen were rattling in the corridor. A day nurse was moving from bed to bed offering pain relief. At her bed the nurse said 'You were running a temperature last night so your surgeon has put you on two different antibiotics.' The nurse put a line in her arm and injected the antibiotics and put a stopper in the line. 'Now there!'

A woman with the breakfast trolley came in. She asked for tea and toast. She sat up in bed and held the cup of tea to her chest. Mustn't spill on her hospital gown.

A man in a suit walked in with a group of young acolytes. By his confident mien and stance she could tell he was a surgeon. Her surgeon. He had his hand in his trouser pocket and rattled what sounded like car keys, the sound of a busy man with a big car. He cleared his throat and turned to his students. 'This seventy-two-year old lady attended A&E yesterday with pain in the right lower quadrant... suspected appendicitis...ultrasound indicated a mass in her colon... secondaries in her liver... I decided to do open surgery to remove a piece of the infarcted omentum. and...'

She stopped listening. A mass! She knew the euphemisms, a mass, a thickening, a lesion, shadow. Say it, she thought, say the word *Cancer!* Secondaries in my liver! Jesus wept!

'Any questions?' A student put his hand up. He was told to look up 'omentum' in Basic Anatomy. Just for devilment she decided to ask the surgeon what an omentum was. He turned to her and said it was belly fat. He put his hand on his own stomach. 'We all have it', he smiled at her. Top marks for bedside manner. They left.

She lay back and looked at the ceiling. There was nothing up there. So she was riddled with Cancer! It had finally caught up with her like it had with so many of her generation comrades. She was seventy-two, called 'vulnerable and elderly' during the pandemic. She thought of the six stages people went through when given bad news. Despair, denial, anger, bargaining, depression and then acceptance. All the stages were coming at her like a tsunami.

She rolled over to her side and managed to get her legs down the side of the bed and got on her feet. With difficulty she walked out to the corridor. It looked endless and was lined with the bland pictures of blurry bouquets of flowers and indifferent landscapes. But over the double doors there was a life size woodcarving of the crucified Christ. The brutality of it was almost a blessed relief. No offence, Jesus!

At the end of the corridor she sat down on a plastic chair beside the lifts. A recorded English voice kept saying 'Going down, doors closing' over and over from the lift shaft. The tape must have got stuck. She should plan her funeral to pass the time she had left. It would save her daughter the bother. But first of all she would clear out her house and get rid of a lifetime of junk and take all unnecessary clothes to charity shops. Then she had to get decent pyjamas and nightdresses and two good dressing gowns. Nothing frivolous, just functional with big pockets. Maybe like artists' smocks? Soon it would be permanent bedtime for her. But first she had to put her affairs in order, set up standing orders, sign a power of attorney for her daughter. For the funeral she would choose an off-the-peg religious service. No point reinventing the wheel. She wanted a professional singer to belt out 'Be Still my Soul'. Make the guests cry, not a dry eye in the house. Afterwards there would be a gathering in a hired function room with food and tango music. Not the Argentinean kind, it would have to be Finnish tango. She had heard Finnish tango music many years ago when she went with her husband to a medical conference in a coastal town in Finland. Every afternoon at five there was a tea dance for pensioners. Eighty-year-olds walked around to tango music in a minor key holding on to each other. The scene had looked like a melancholy dance of death. The participants knew the steps and moves and seem to enjoy it.

Thinking about her funeral didn't make death seem any more real. Was she in denial? She went back to the ward to lie down and look at the ceiling. She pressed the buttons beside the bed. Bed going up! Going down! Great invention.

More days passed. The surgeon came in with his students, all of them wearing little white coats. They all kept their eyes fixed on the surgeon and laughed when he laughed. Sometimes they glanced at her and then tactfully averted their eyes. When they were about to leave the surgeon turned to one of the students and said 'Book a colonoscopy for tomorrow for this lady! And an MRI of the the liver as soon as possible!' He made a backwards jerk of his head as if to say 'Make it so' and turned on his heel and walked away with the boys. Why had he picked the only girl for the task? Now the girl would miss out on something that would come up in the next exam. The girl put her fists into the pockets of her white coat and said 'Eh...I better see to that so.' She ran away with her white coat flapping behind her.

After the colonoscopy she was back on the ward and the surgeon came in. 'Good news! No mass was found in your bowel. Now we will just run a few tests and do an MRI of your liver. But not to worry, dear, you're in good hands!'

When she was back home she pottered around her house and emptied boxes of old toys, old albums, old bills, old tax returns, old everything. It was an absorbing task and mentally very taxing. She remembered sorting her husband's clothes after he died when she cried over every shirt and tie, every pair of shoes. It took six months. This had to be faster.

The day for the MRI came. She had to tick YES or NO on a list of items not compatible with magnetic resonance imaging. Anything made of metal had to be declared. Pacemakers, shrapnel in the body, welding sparks in the eyes, metal plates, stents, hip replacements, bullets. She ticked NO to everything. Final question: 'Are you claustrophobic?' Answer: NO. I like dark enclosed spaces.

Then it was time to go into to the steel tube, the mighty sarcophagus. She lay down on the narrow bed and crossed her arms Pharaoh-style but was told to put her arms down. The nurse handed her a panic button that she could press.

'Keep your eyes closed, it'll make it easier', the nurse said. She was rolled into the machine that would prophesise her future. She hadn't expected the sound of panel beaters going hell for leather at the steel tube and the sound of a circular saw from hell cutting her midriff into thin salami slices. She asked the radiologist for the result and was told it was for her doctor to say.

When she got home she set to clearing her house with more haste than before.

No time to lose now. She had an appointment to see the surgeon in two weeks. She had to hurry before it was too late.

When she walked into the surgeon's room he sat behind his desk reading a letter. When he looked up and saw her there, he stood up and held his hand out across the desk. She shook it. They sat down. He cleared his throat 'I have here the report from the radiologist. It shows a number of areas of irregularities in your liver. We have conferred and come to the conclusion that they are benign cysts of no importance.' She looked at him blankly. She wanted doctors to be super-human. This one wasn't super-human, he was only pretending because a surgeon has to be incisive. The hand that holds the scalpel mustn't tremble. He stood up and came around the desk and hurried her to the door, putting a reassuring palm between her shoulder blades. 'Does that mean I don't have cancer?' she said. He harrumphed 'I just said, dear! Go home and pour yourself a stiff gin and tonic! Good bye now!'

On the way back home she dropped into the charity shop where she had donated her dresses. She rifled through the rail of unloved, back of the wardrobe smelling, frocks. She found the dress that she had donated the previous week, her best dress that she had kept in lavender-scented tissue paper for special occasions. Now priced at €8. She bought it.

Outside the shop she smiled to herself and did a little hop and skip. There's life in the old girl still! She would wear the dress at the tea dance she would have for family and friends.

Evelyn Conlon

Reasons I Know of That We Are Not Allowed to Speak to Our Grandmother

It began with me having to do an essay for school about my grandmother. Only some of us were asked to do it. It was for a competition for a visiting writer who was coming to our class the following month.

'Is that all he does Sir, write?' a boy asked.

'Yes, that's what he is, a writer, just like your father is an actuary, I believe.'

That may have been the first time the boy had a name for what his father was.

Those of us who were chosen made a show of huffing and puffing and told the others that they were lucky, but secretly I was pleased. The essay was to be about how the old spent their Saturday nights. Mr. McGrane was particularly interested in how those who lived alone fared on such a busy evening. He must have chosen those of us who had grannies living on their own, maybe it was not because we were good at essays. We could concentrate on aspects of loneliness. Were they more poignant in contrast to the fullness of the clamour and clatter of a Saturday night? P O I G N A N T. We could look it up in the dictionary. And while we were at it, we could find out the difference between 'bathos' and 'pathos'. The ones who weren't chosen laughed at that and some of them pointed their fingers at us. Mr. McGrane saw that, and said that everyone had to look up the words.

'And I would like you to stick as near to the truth as possible'

It was this commandment that made me niggle my father over and over again that evening and the next day to bring me to our grandmother's at 9 o'clock on Saturday night. That was not a time that we would normally visit her. I had decided on 9 o'clock because I thought that the loneliness mentioned by Mr.McGrane would have set in by then, and I'd be able to see it for myself, without my grandmother or my father knowing what I was up to.

When we arrived at the door she wasn't in and my father seemed annoyed by this. We puttered about for a while but she didn't come back.

'Are you sure Mr. Mc.Grane meant you to be so precise? Seems more like a report to me than an essay. Surely an essay should be more imaginative.'

I hated it when my father got all know all like that. As if he knew better than my teacher. I said, bolstered by the order to accuracy, 'Yes.'

'Oh well then, we'd better look for her, I suppose' my father said.

We went next door to my grandmother's neighbour, an old woman who scared me the way that I think grandmothers are maybe meant to, but which mine didn't. My father asked her if she might know where my grandmother was.

'What time is it? That blooming clock is never right'

This struck me as odd; surely there would be more than one clock in the house. Ours had at least four that I could think of at this minute. Maybe I would put in the essay that my grandmother's neighbour had only one clock and it was always wrong.

'It's eh… let me see…' and my father pulled back the sleeve of his jacket to look at his watch, which had a purple face. I could hear a baby crying in the house on the other side.

'Half past nine now', he said.

'Half past nine on a Saturday night. Well she'll have her feet well up back in Slatterys by now. Slatterys, you know, the pub.'

My father closed his face. You have to know him well to see him doing that. I know him well, or at least the bits of him that I notice.
'Slatterys, the pub', she said again, putting the emphasis on the last word.
'Yes. Yes' my father said, tetchily, and my grandmother's neighbour chuckled.

'What did she mean *back* in Slatterys?' I asked when we were in the car.

'Oh, she's from the West, they say back with everything.'

My father sounded cross. I was only trying to get him to open his face again.

Maybe if we hadn't gone to the pub it would have been alright. He parked the car in a sullen manner. I would need to look that up too with the bathos word. I hear words and like them but sometimes use them in the wrong place. He said. 'stay there', unnecessarily. Even I knew that children were not allowed in pubs after nine o'clock at night. There had been an uproar about it which I couldn't understand. What could happen that you would have to have a child in a pub after nine o'clock at night? And what was the difference between a pub and a bar? I hadn't brought my book with me; we had, after all, only been going to visit our grandmother. There was nothing to read in the car except some scraps, but they did alright.

My father came out from the pub a few minutes later – I'm not sure exactly how long he was in there but I hadn't got bored. He was fuming. That word is definitely correct. I thought it best not to talk on the way home.

I was sent to bed the minute we got in, unreasonably early, I thought. Later, as the noise from the kitchen got louder, I left my room and sat on the top of the stairs. There is always a child on the stairs, otherwise how would we learn.

'You want to see the crowd she was with.'

'Did you know any of them?'

'Not one. And the way she..'

'Tell me again what she said', my mother interrupted, sounding as if she wanted to put the answer out flat on the table and examine it the way she did before she sewed something.

'She said that I should be grateful she had a life and wasn't sitting at home alone moping about. She said that I had no business checking up on her, that she'd had enough constriction when she was rearing me.'

'Are you sure it was *constriction* she said?'

'Yes I'm sure', my father ground out, 'I would hardly make it up.'

'And did she really ask you to leave?' my mother asked in her kind voice.

'Well as good as.'

The conversation went on like this for a long time, sounding liked turned down music or distant wind, but I couldn't follow it really and also, I did get bored because I couldn't understand what they were getting so exercised about. You can use that word as a description. It does not mean that they have been running or swimming all night.

On Monday when Mr. McGrane asked me how the essay was going I said 'fine.'

It was very soon after that that our grandmother arrived at our house full of high dudgeon – I love when I can think that's what people are in. I'm almost certain that if the pub episode had not happened, we would not have got that visit. This time I was out in the garden, and although my father closed the door – now that I think of it, already not prepared to let things return to normal – I moved up to the back wall and sat down under the open window. My older sister was getting married, next year I think. There was a lot of fuss, even already, I'd heard my mother saying. Sometimes it would last for an entire hour but then it would die down for days. Sometimes there would be the word wedding, wedding, wedding blowing up all over the place. And then there would be weeks when no-one at all mentioned the circus, as my mother called it. I didn't care about the ins and outs of it, but I presumed it would be interesting to be a part of it on the actual day. It was also a very long way away so I could see no reason to think about it yet. So it surprised me that our grandmother arrived so early to discuss it. Although I'm sure this could not really be called a discussion.

'As you are well aware, I have no interest in ribbons, so clearly I'll be having some trouble with this', our grandmother said. She must then have thrown something on the table, a letter or a card. I don't know if she gave my parents time to finish reading it – there was quiet for a very short time. 'Now I know that there are sewers in the world, people who sew' – even I knew that this was a dig at my mother – 'but they don't have to stick needles into everything'

'Just a minute', my father said.

'Yes', our grandmother said, letting the word turn up at the end, as if it was a question or being said by an Australian.

'Just a minute', my father repeated, 'this is no way to talk to my wife'

'Oh for heaven's sake, Liam, your *what*, she has a name, and actually I'm not just talking to Gertrude, I'm talking to you too. You may not be allowed to say that your daughter has lost the complete run of herself but I can. I will not, I repeat, will not, be told by anyone what to wear, and no-one will ask me to put a ribbon on a hat. Who said I was going to wear a hat anyway?'

'I don't think she meant it like that', my mother said.

'And may I ask what way you think she meant it? This is quite clear. An order to wear a specific colour so that I can fit into some ludicrous pattern that this young one has in mind.'

'But is there anything wrong with the colours matching on the day?' my mother asked.

My father had gone quiet.

'No, indeed there's not, if it so happens that they do. But that's the point, if it so happens.'

Clearly our grandmother was trying to show some interest but I could tell that she didn't care about colours at all. And just then my father piped up, 'This isn't about colours at all, is it Mother? This is about your attitude to marriage.'

Whoa, that was some leap.

I could feel the silence, even outside, and the leg that was under my other one went funny.

'Maybe you're right', our grandmother finally said. 'If you must know, and I think you're old enough now to be able to bear it, I do have serious difficulties with marriage. I think it's something that should be done privately and not particularly referred to again unless legally necessary.'

She sounded as if she was on a home run.

'If you remember, I never referred to your father as my husband until he died, and if you'll care to remember, this had no bearing on what I felt about or for him.'

'Your trouble is that you have no respect for tradition,' my father said.

'Tradition my arse.'

'Look, there's no need to be so rude.'

'Oh grow up, that's not being rude.'

It was funny hearing someone tell my father to grow up. I had to scratch myself so that I wouldn't be found under the window.

There was a moment's silence, as if our grandmother realized the futility of it all. I had looked up 'futility' the night before. It sounded too as if they were all waiting to see who would go next.

My mother then said, 'Could you not just – ' but our grandmother interrupted in a soft voice, 'No, I could not just anything. This is what principle means. Someone has to stand up to this...'

She didn't finish the sentence, as if even she knew that the next word out of her mouth could be too dangerous.

'And as for tradition, these days anything can be made up into it. It could be something started five years ago. Any old gobshite in a bar could tell them it was always done and they'd believe him.'

'You'd know all about that.'

I didn't know if it was fair of my father to say that. My grandmother then changed her voice into the sort of a one that my mother sometimes uses on us, only us. It comes from outside the sound of normal conversation.

'In this tradition of yours', our grandmother said, 'I see that maternal respect has got the push.'

It sounded as if she was just at the beginning of her sentence but my father interrupted in the voice that he uses on the telephone if someone rings from work – everyone was changing voices now – 'I'm sorry you feel like that. Do you want a lift anywhere?'

I could hear him coming towards the window so I had to creep my way across to the hedge and slip behind the coal shed away out of sight. It's not used as a coal shed any more since we got the natural gas. Everything is thrown into it. I didn't hear the car leaving.

At tea time the faces were all closed.

And that night when I went out on the stairs, I could hear a real ding-dust of a shouting match. When their voices get that way, they wouldn't notice me even if they tripped over me. The shoutings all ran into each other and it was hard to make out where one began and the other ended, but I did hear plainly my mother saying,

'Your mother was always the same. Happy away up there on her high horse. I'm not surprised she has ended up ...' I couldn't hear the next bit.

'And as for these views of hers. Always superior in her mind to everyone else. Could never have the same look on things as everyone else. Oh no, Miss Precious.'

She was talking about our grandmother!

'There was no call for that, no call at all,' my father shouted.

I had to agree with him. I heard a door slamming, saw a slice of light land on the banisters and knew that someone was going to make towards the hall, and in truth too I had decided that it was best for me to hear no more anyway. I slid my bottom across the linoleum into my bedroom. My mother had changed all the upstairs carpet for linoleum – I liked the colour of that word – she said it was healthier. You could never tell the connections that some people make, they must think a lot to come up with them.

The following weekend I was taken away by my parents to the west and we all had a very smooth time, people holding hands and all that.

On Monday Mr.McGrane asked me how the essay was going and I said 'Fine Sir.'

He also said that, in the opinion of some, Wittgenstein tried to destroy philosophy because he could not understand it. There is no point in destroying something if you don't know what it is. Then again, for many, that's why they destroy things, precisely because they do not know their worth. I hope you got that. Some of you may need to know it. And he destroyed Mr. Russell too.' Whoever he was.

I am already a perhaps sort of person. Perhaps everything would have gone completely back to normal if my essay had not won the competition. And been printed in the local paper. Oh Shite. I can say that out loud because my parents seem to have too much else on their minds to notice and to reprimand me. I got a postcard from my grandmother congratulating me and that seems to have let all hell loose altogether. But my father did say yesterday, 'See, I told you an imaginative approach is always best.' The fact that he referred to it at all makes me think that his face might open again, and that I'll be able to speak to my grandmother some day soon.

from *Moving About the Place* (Belfast: Blackstaff Press, 2021)

Lia Mills

How long has it been?

'Lean back.'

The voice comes from behind her, through a brassy jangle of Christmas muzak, hairdryers, loud conversation. Stylists all in black but for cheery red-and-white santa hats. They chat to their reflections in the mirrored wall over the papered, crimped, dyeing heads of their clients. A row of women alongside Ciss on this side of the salon are laid out like fish on a slab, heads tilted back into basins, legs up on the new feature Sandy, who owns the place, is so proud of: recliners with little moving parts that are meant to massage your back. They only annoy Ciss, so she says, Leave it off. They'd remind her of sunbathing beside a hotel swimming pool but there's no blue sky here. It's raining pigs outside.

She lifts her neck and looks into the mirrors across the way for a glimpse of her girl, the one who spoke, the one who'll wash her hair today. She's only gone and left her glasses in her bag but she can just about make out a blondey wisp of a thing with a pale face, hoops of silver at her ears. She's waiting. Water's running. Ciss tips her head back into a basin shaped like a halter for a carthorse, gives it over to the young one's unseen hands. She pushes the porcelain collar deeper onto Ciss's shoulders, gathers what remains to Ciss of hair and runs a hose over it. The hair has started coming out in clumps. Enough catches on her brush in the mornings to stuff a mattress, the drain in the shower is vile. Stress, the most likely cause. All the stress she's under. Milo, losing his mind. That bitch Ben married. She has no shortage of hair, wears it wild and tangled-looking, gypsy. Going grey. Nothing ages a woman like grey hair, Ciss tells her, for all the good it does. Might as well talk to the mirror over there.

'Water alright?'

'Unh.' Flat on her back now, Ciss stares at the ceiling: Dirty grey squares of something industrial. Why don't they put something interesting up there to look at? She keeps meaning to say it to Sandy but then she forgets until the next time she's stuck here like this, looking up. Water runs warm across her scalp. Delicious. The young one lifts and drops handfuls of wet hair. Could she not show a bit of interest? The pretence of it, even? The hose clatters to the sink then there's the chemical-sweet smell of shampoo. Strong young fingers return to rummage through the roots of Ciss's hair with deep circular movements. Bliss.

Her eyes slide shut. She was wound tight as a clock when she came in here but this one has clever fingers, she'll give her that. A curling pressure at the roots of her hair loosens her shoulders, eases a tension in her neck she hadn't known was there. Her breath is shallow, she could doze off any minute. *Relax.* When was the last time she was touched by someone who wasn't paid to do it? She shoots upright. Water sprays everywhere.

'What? Did I burn you?'

'Never mind.' Ciss settles back, but the mood is spoiled. Her ribs are clenched worse than before. It's true. Hair, nails, the odd massage Ben and that bitch of a daughter-in-law used give her vouchers for at Christmas, anniversaries, birthdays. She put a stop to it herself. She's past all that now, bar the nails. Arthritis or not, she prefers to do those herself.

And the hair. You have to have a little dignity, wherever you can find it. The list lengthens in her head: physio. Chiropody. Always something to pay for.

Head massage over, she asks for a treatment. The young one slathers some unguent onto the hair, wraps Ciss's head in a warm towel, says she'll be back in a sec and disappears. The pure note of a boy soprano pierces the brassy jitter and chatter in the place. *Once in Royal David's City.* Ciss shivers. There are sounds that do that to her, pierce the back of her throat. It doesn't mean anything. She lets her head rest back on the folded towel the young one left and dips her chin to see across the salon. A row of backs (all women) tented in sheets of grey plastic to catch hair and colourant and what, these days, they call *product*. Beyond the women and their tortured hair, reflections avoid their own eyes, their altered faces. Interesting, the effect of scraping a person's hair back off her face and twisting it into squares of white paper, or layering it with paste, or twisting it up into strange loops parked at odd angles, while someone wields a dryer around them. Nowhere to hide. Like bald men.

No, not like them at all. Men are different.

The women across the way flick through magazines or watch their stylist's reflection at work, or look at screens balanced in their laps. Hair glooped, crimped, pinned, brushed-up and back-combed or dragged ceilingwards between a brush and the nozzle of a dryer. In the corner an oval, neon tube swivels slowly around the bent head of a woman writing a list on the back of an envelope. Ciss approves. Any sign of mobile phone resistance is a good thing, in her book.

Stylists come and go. The phone rings, off and on. The receptionist makes appointments, takes in coats, gives others back. Ciss's head swims. Between muzak and hunger and the smells of the place there's some slippage in her mind. It's like all those other women across the way are versions of herself. That one and that one and that one are Ciss and Ciss and Ciss at different ages and stages of life, all here, having their hair done every which way, any old way, none. Makes Ciss want to scream out but – *Don't*, she tells herself. *Don't do it. Keep Sandy onside.* A bored child pushes a sweeping brush along the floor gathering curls and shavings and blunt chopped chunks of hair, all shades and textures. Her thighs strain against too-tight stretch-denim jeggings. She could be Ciss too, only younger – but for the oblong shape of a phone visible through her pocket – toasting her ovaries, if she only knew – and the lovely skin on her, the two-tone gold-on-red shade of her hair. The one who's slipped out for a smoke – who Ciss can clearly see out the shopfront window because she's forgotten herself and is pacing, gesticulating, arguing with someone right there in full view – shouldn't be allowed – she could be Ciss too, talking to either of her own ungrateful cold-hearted children. *What about me?*

She lies back again, closes her eyes and drifts. Behind her, low voices. A laugh. Her young one is back, telling the one at the next basin a story. For all Ciss knows, it's her they're laughing at. There's the ceiling, still. Fluorescent bars of light fixed to squares of grey plasterboard. A smoke alarm. Telltale nicotiney stains here and there hint at damp and old leaks. The tops of the mirrors are draped with red and silver tinsel. Ciss's girl rolls her head to one side, scrubs, then the other side, scrubs again. The hose runs. A fresh towel is wrapped around her head and she's led across the floor to the station where she sat before. Now the young one asks if she'd like anything, teacoffeewater? A bit late to be so solicitous. Ciss isn't fooled. *No tip for you, Miss.*

The woman at the station next to Ciss flips the pages of *Hello* magazine, scanning the photographs, as if she's likely to have heard of anyone in them, bar the Royals. As though she feels Ciss looking, she nudges the stack of mags beyond reach. Ciss doesn't want them. She wants the half bar of Galaxy from the bottom of her own bag but – she takes another look at your woman again, at the fold of excess skin that puckers her elbow where it comes out from under the salon's gown. Better not.

The so-familiar Christmas tracks batter her ears. At last Sandy, her stylist, appears beside her, rummaging in a drawer full of brushes. The hair of other clients is caught in the bristles, a purplish light in the drawer the only suggestion that they could be – should be – in any way sterile.

'How do you stand that racket?' Ciss asks.

'Don't even hear it any more. Back in a sec.' And off Sandy goes in search of a different brush. Ciss is glad she doesn't have to see the tangle it emerges from, if it's coming for her.

Everything is as it always is: the brushing and the blowing dry, the tipping and the paying (*don't think about it, don't*) the finding of the coat and the *See-you-next-times*, except that Ciss's mind has darkened, as though a lightbulb's blown in there, or a fuse.

She carries her body outside with this new shadow or cast around it, like one of those chalk lines they draw around a murdered corpse in films. She's aware of her*self*, separate from her body, like a mahout perched up high on a howdah while her elephantine self ambles along below.

The skin on her hands, knees and elbows has thickened into roundy sworls that are, no denying it, elephantine. The image of that other woman's elbow comes back like the warning it is. All around her, wherever she looks, she sees fat on other people. Rolls of it. Stomachs swell and bulge. Pillowed arms. A term she'd forgotten – thunder thighs – comes back to her, looking at all the people poured into clothes too small for them. *Beef to the heel like a Mullingar heifer.* Girls and women in black leggings that might as well be tights, they're that sheer. Does no one ever tell them their underwear is clear as day? Or else they're dressed like that bitch, her son's wife: tented layers supposed to conceal unruly flesh but adding to it instead. Shoals of women, overweight, overripe, softening. Ready to rot if not rotten already.

Ciss has always been on the big side, no getting away from it. Tall. Big-boned. She suffered for it in taunts at school from the likes of Lyddie O'Meara but she had known herself to be statuesque, on a different scale than her companions. And Milo, in better times, had liked her body so thoroughly she learned to like it too.

The memory makes her smile. Those were days alright. She catches the eye of the young busker at the post-box and he smiles back. Ciss fishes a euro coin from her pocket and drops it into his open guitar case then wishes she hadn't. She wishes her fingers had closed on something smaller and besides, it's turned his gorgeous smile into one more thing she's had to pay for.

(Extract from *Harpy*, a novel-in-progress)

Celia De Fréine

His Ice Creamio is the Bestio

Yankee doodle came to town riding on a pony.
He stuck a feather up his arse and called it macaroni.
Yankee doodle keep it up. Yankee doodle dandy.
Man the guns upon the shore and treat the girls with candy.

Not many Yanks hereabouts. Not many of anyone. Apart from in the bar. Clive and Romney. Whenever I get in to see them, which isn't often. She sees to that. With her rules and regulations. And her house in Raytown. On the south bank of Dublin City. What a place to fetch up in. A ray of what, I thought first time I heard tell of it.

It means fish. Like the ones in the aquarium. Most fish give me the creeps. The way they look at you. With those eyes of theirs. Especially when they're served up on a plate. The ray in the aquarium were sashaying in the water. Like ghosts in a chorus line. And they were pretty. Prettier than any ghost I've seen. And I've seen a few in my day. Starting with the ones that rose up out of that air raid rubble during the blitz. Up North, the place I come from. The ghosts of a woman and her baby. Up they floated, up and away.

I didn't ask to live here. In Mum's house. Mum is my daughter. Francesca, to give her her proper name. Boys used to pick on her in school, so she shortened it to Fran. Then, as soon as her own wean, Alannah began to talk, everyone called her Mum. I wanted to honour her heritage – that's why I chose Francesca. But I couldn't tell anyone, least of all my husband, Michael.

She's down in the kitchen now and I'm up here in bed. While we take a break from the celebrations. Alannah, who's turned out well, in spite of Mum, is conked out on the couch. And her wean, Saoirse, is asleep in her pram. We've just watched a programme on the BBC. The bringing in of the new year – the way they do it in Scotland. Hog-malony. The new millennium it is this time.

When we're rested we'll get up to see the sun rise over Dublin Bay. Mum's on the phone to her boyfriend. A boyfriend, at her age. Who'd have thought it, with her pushing sixty? Another boring academic. Like herself. She'll be telling him all about her book. Who needs to know what kind of knickers they wore in the nineteenth century?

She fancies herself and himself will head off on a tour of historic sites come spring. After she's dumped me. Let her think what she likes. Even if she did get rid of me, there's Alannah to think of. And she's one feisty wee woman.

We had some fun today, all the same, Alannah and me. After we escaped down to the bar. Promised we'd get ice cream for the baked alaska. Then forgot all about it. How those hot toddies warmed me up. Three of them I knocked back. Clive bought one. Then Romney. Then Alannah. Mum was mad when we got back. She started on about the ice cream. How can I make a baked alaska without ice cream, she said. I've spent hours separating the white of six eggs to make the meringue. We'll take it neat, Alannah said.

How many has *she* had, Mum asked Alannah. Like it was any of her business. She had three as well. Cognacs hers were. I like a woman who knows her spirits. Thank God she gave up the breastfeeding. Who needs a wean hanging out of her morning, noon and night? Not Alannah, for sure. She has more to be doing. Like working on her film. A documentary on war brides. She was out in one of those foreign countries last year. What's this the name of it was? Interviewing soldiers' wives.

The three hot toddies will have to do me for a while. Unless Alannah manages to smuggle some booze into the house. I'd choose it over the pills any time. Rather than spend the rest of my days spaced out like a zombie. Nor do the fags do me any harm either. I managed to get four off the guys in the bar. But Mum found them in my pocket and confiscated them. Said she didn't want me setting fire to the place again. What if I did? It could do with a makeover. Mum has that furniture since she married your man, Lar. Such a pity it didn't all go up in flames last time. I wasn't to know she'd left a tissue covered in nail varnish in the bin when I threw in my butt.

She doesn't know what it is to suffer. To go bare-legged in winter. I told Alannah about that. How, when the war was on and we had no stockings, we had to draw a line with a lead pencil up the back of our legs all the way up to our drawers. To make it look like a seam. She put that in her film. Why the fuck am I going off to these foreign countries, Gran, she said, when I have a war bride here in my own home? It isn't her home, though. No more than I'm a war bride.

I reckon her plan is to move back in. Herself and Saoirse. What kind of a name is that, anyhow? That's what comes of Alannah going to live in the Gaeltock with her Dad when she was seven. When she chose him over Mum. And could you blame her? Which parent would you choose? An academic with her nose in a book or a man with a sail boat?

That's where she met Garry. We went down to the wedding on the train.

Me and Mum. One hundred and seventy guests were at it. Alannah spent the whole day telling Garry she loved him. In front of everyone. In a dress that dress cost two grand. Slobbering over him. Kiss. Kiss. Slobber. Slobber. And the big house they built. A hacienda Mum calls it. Turns out Garry wanted Alannah all to himself. That's the problem with men. They want to take over your life. Even if they dump you they still take it over. Cos you spend your days trying to figure out why they dumped you. The women on the telly eat tubs of ice cream when they get dumped. I did too. At first. I wonder about Clive and Romney, all the same. Best to keep them at arm's length. I like that they were soldiers. And went out foreign to take on Mr Hitler. Too bad they got blacklisted for their trouble.

Garry drove all the way up here this afternoon. He phoned Mum to say he was going to throw himself in the canal unless Alannah came back home with him. Just as well it happened when we were in the bar. Alannah and me. She'd forgotten to bring her phone. On purpose, I shouldn't wonder. Smart woman. And Mum had to drive over to the Canal Dock with the wean in the back seat to try to talk him down. But he wasn't having any. Even the sight of the wean wasn't enough to put him off. Lucky for him the coastguard came in their dinghy and fished him out of the water. And carted him off to the loony bin. That should shut him up for a while.

As for Lar, Alannah's father, I managed to get rid of him. Back when Alannah was a wean. I could see how much he was scundering Mum. And when I got the insurance money after Michael died I gave it to him and told him to go west and buy a boat. Mum never suspected a thing until it all came out today at the dinner. She nearly choked on a prawn in her seafood cocktail when she heard. That's the thing about the festive season, it's great for stirring things up. And there's more to come. The biggest shitstorm in living memory is about to hit the fan. After we get up, pull back the curtains and stand at the window to watch the light spread out behind the stripey poles of the power-station. I'll tell them when we're laying into our Ulster Fry. Alannah can put it in her film.

I already told her most things. About how the Americans, Sebastiano and Bruce, came when the war was half over. They were sent to man the guns in the bunkers and keep Mr Hitler from invading Ulster. The two of them brought Camel cigarettes and nylon stockings. Nylon was newly invented then.

As for our clothes, it was make-do and mend. Alannah was pleased I was wearing burgundy today. Like the burgundy suit I had back then. There was an elderly woman living near us, a Protestant, Mrs McKibben. I used to bring her her tea and sugar and whatever she was entitled to on her rations. She took pity on me cos I was honest and didn't short change her. One day she handed me a pair of curtains. Burgundy they were. Covered in dust. I hear you're handy with a needle, she said.

When I got home I spread them out on the table. They were faded around the edges and there was a wee rip in one of them but they were that big I could work around the rip and faded bits. There was enough for a jacket and a skirt. Even taking into account they were velvet and the pile had to go all one way. The skirt was short. That was the fashion then. They used to say I had nice legs. I'd no stockings, though. Until I met him. Sebastiano.

Alannah's film is in Gaelic. That's what they talk in the Gaeltock. I can't talk Gaelic, I said to her. But I know what An Lár means. It's where all the buses go when you can't get one. She says she'll translate my story into Gaelic and do a voiceover. Who'd have thought I'd be a film star at my age? Not that I care to remember what that is, so long as I can draw my pension every Friday.

We always wore clean underwear. Me and my friend, Madge. In case a bomb landed on top of us. One with our name on it. We would rinse our bits and pieces the night before. I had two pairs of drawers. And two camisoles. Silk. One dove grey. The other eau-de-Nil. And a suspender belt in a pale shade of ivory. She was a nurse and I was a shorthand typist.

I was wearing the burgundy suit the day I met Sebastiano. A dab of powder, scraped from the bottom of the compact on my nose and cheekbones. Lippy from crushed blackberries on my beak. That looks nice, he said. We got chatting. And met most days after that when he was off duty and someone else was keeping an eye out for Mr Hitler. Sebastiano and his pal, Bruce, and me and Madge, would go for tea in the café in the railway station. The wee man in the café would say, high tea or low? Lifting the teapot up and down. And Madge would say, would you have any preserves, Mr McConchie? That means jam. Alannah says I'm a walking encyclopedia.

You can be sure what I have to say is more interesting than what Mum's writing in that book of hers. She's keen to get it finished. What's the hurry, I said. None of the facts are going to change. Only she's afraid her mortal enemy, a one with a face on her like a hard boiled egg, is going to steal a march. Mum reckons she stole her idea and it's a race to the finish. And they're neck and neck as they round the bend. One furlong to go and hard-boiled-egg-face is gaining on Mum. They're past the post now. And Mum has won by a nose. Yippee.

When the war was over me and Michael and Mum migrated down here to the Free State. At first it seemed worth it. There was no end to the big floury spuds smothered in butter. Mr Dee-Val-Éire said the people of Ulster were Irish. Such a load of baloney. My Michael spent the best years of his life slaving away. Earning half nothing. Just like those wee Indian boys down in Spar.

As for Sebastiano. With his big brown eyes. You'd run away with him. If only. Those days it was eat, drink and be merry for tomorrow we die. But we lived to tell the tale. Plenty of jobs in the North after the war. If you dug with the foot that mattered.

Bruce wrote to Madge and proposed to her. Asked her to sail off to America. Make a new life for herself there. She didn't want to go. I said to her there's more to life in America than Camel cigarettes and nylon stockings. Think of the skyscrapers. That's what I am thinking of, she said. I'm afraid one them them might topple over and fall down on top of me. What a thing to say. And the two of us having come through that air raid without a scratch. Madge wanted to feel safe. And she did. For a while. She and her dope of a husband set up a wee hardware business up North. And were doing well enough until they got blew up by a bomb. One that had their name on it. And it wasn't one of Mr Hitler's neither.

I can't wait to lay in to the fried potato cake. And the wheaten and soda farls. That's when I'll tell Alannah and Mum about Sebastiano. I hope I can remember the facts as clear as I can now. One thing I'm in no doubt about: when Sebastiano went back to America he wrote to me and said:

> *I love you, Eithne, but our love is not to be.*
> *I am at home now. With my family.*
> *And you are far away. Across the sea.*

That was how he dumped me. I read his letter over and over. Then I walked down to the shore. In the town where I grew up. I wonder are the bunkers still there. And wandered into the ice cream parlour. The man who owned it was Italian. Just like Sebastiano.

> *Dino Cabrellio, he sells ice creamio.*
> *His ice creamio is the bestio.*

A lovely man. Gave me a vanilla sundae when he noticed the tears streaming down my cheeks. Ice cream always reminds me of that day. When I was so hurt I wanted to throw myself under the next train. Dino suspecting as much. Telling me to take my time. To eat as many sundaes as I wanted. As if he was used to seeing young pregnant women jilted. As if it happened every day of the week.

Phyl Herbert

Lunar Ladies

Her trolley is laid. The cups are placed upside down on saucers stacked on plates, ready for the action of the afternoon. Sundays at Annie's is an event written into the social calendar of many women of her acquaintance. But this Sunday is different, it is the Sunday before the New Year and only two women are invited. The bottom shelf of the trolley hides the sweet delicacies that will follow the egg sandwiches. She looks in the big gilt framed mirror, pins back the curl on her forehead with a silver slide and then adjusts her dark glasses. She scans her figure from head to toe. Annie is wearing her favourite dress given to her by her best friend Hilda. A knitted dress of deep royal blue fits snugly on her four foot ten inch frame. The pink pom-poms complete the outfit. She smiles at her reflection. The doorbell rings. 'Coming', she hums. She lifts the buzzer phone on the wall of her living room, opening the door to the apartment block. She is standing at her living room door when Hilda arrives. 'Hope I'm not too early?', she kisses Annie on the cheek.

'Delighted to see you Hilda, I'm more than ready.' Hilda places her fur coat behind the white settee. She hands Annie a small box – 'a few eclairs for later.'

The table in the centre of the room is covered with paper cuttings of theatre reviews. The bell rings again and Annie lifts the buzzer phone and says 'come in if you're good looking.' Bonnie enters.

'We're all here now.' Annie says, 'that time of year thou mayst in me behold.' Annie makes this pronouncement as if she were about to say Mass.

'You look terrific Bonnie, your hair is getting blonder and you are getting younger looking, I swear to God, I don't know what you're doing to yourself.' Hilda says almost accusingly.

Bonnie looks in the mirror and chuckles. 'I have to say folks I'm sorry I didn't do all this years ago, whoever said youth is wasted on the young was right.'

'You're dead right there Bonnie sure when we were young we were good looking girls and didn't know it. What sort of eejits were we?' Hilda asks.

'Are you still playing tennis Bonnie?' Annie asks looking up at Bonnie re-applying her red lipstick.

'Yes, Annie, I was playing this morning actually. I play with three other women and they would beat any young player off the court. Hard to believe they are in their seventies. They still have power in their elbows and strength in their swing. Their legs are not as good obviously, like my own, they won't always obey the head, but the skill and style shines through.

'How often do you play with them Bonnie?'

'Twice a week, I'd play more often if I could but sure tennis is like sex. You can't do it alone.'

She looks at Annie for a response, she is warming up, trying a few shots. Annie smiles and lifts her small shoulders and plays back to Bonnie. Annie may be small but she likes to project large.

'Age is all about confidence.' Annie is projecting again. She mulls over her words.

'Look at that director fellow, he must be in his sixties going out with that young one. His own daughters are older than her.'

Hilda is on the edge of her seat. 'Go on', she urges Annie to continue. Hilda has seen two husbands to the grave. 'Sure I didn't live at all, got no pleasure out of any of them.'

The three women sit in the centre of the living room. The apartment was left to Annie by her aunt and uncle forty years ago. They were both Abbey actors and the room is a shrine to their memory. Framed photographs line up a gallery of remembrances. The walls are green, theatre green. The acting heroes look down from every side of the room. Three white sofas surround the low table where Annie collects her reviews and writes her daily diary.

'Well Annie, what did you see at the Theatre Festival this year?' Annie takes a breath and rises in the chair. 'The Crucible, it was bleak, I left at the interval.'

Bonnie is surprised, she too had seen it. 'My God Annie, not again, you didn't go back after the interval?'

'No. I couldn't hear that fellow who played the father, he couldn't project, actors can't project anymore.'

'I don't know Annie, I enjoyed it, I think Arthur Miller is the master playwright, none of those young playwrights know how to write a play, they're all full of the rambling monologues.'

Bonnie knew the theatre scene in Dublin, she spent most of her youth directing other peoples' talents. It was now her time. She had written a poem to herself entitled 'Archaeology of the Soul', nobody but herself will see it.

ARCHAEOLOGY OF THE SOUL

At the funeral of my youth
Only one offered a cushioned grave for my remains.
'Will you marry me?' He asked
I was thirty then and on the shelf
'No, I replied and then I died.
Now I'm the big OH...
And have opened up myself on the shelf.
I want to dance to the tune of sex
Have babies and catch up with myself.

Annie rises from her seat and goes into the kitchen. She is about to perform the tea ritual. Hilda looks at Bonnie and smiles, 'We have to let her, it is her party.'

'How did your Christmas go Hilda'? 'Mother of God, I'm glad it's all over, I was stuck in a corner at my niece's table and I thought I'd never get home.' Hilda is breathless, 'Do you know what they gave me? A single cup and saucer wrapped up in fancy paper with a blooming big bow on it. Now if that is not a reminder that I live alone, I don't know what is? I can't wait for the New Year.'

Annie comes back pushing her trolley to the centre of the room. Hilda places the three cups upwards on their saucers and Bonnie pours the tea. The egg sandwiches are eaten and as always someone says, 'Annie, you make the best egg sandwiches in Ireland.'

The fancy cake plates at the bottom of the trolley are decked with Hilda's chocolate eclairs and Bonnie's Swiss Roll. Both have to be sampled. Hilda takes a bite of chocolate eclair and looks at Annie, 'It's only here Annie that I allow myself the pleasure.'

Did you see Nigella last night?' Annie asks.

'No, what was she cooking?' Bonnie enquires.

'I don't give a fig for what she cooks', Annie says indignantly, 'I just love looking at the sheer physicality of her performance, she makes me feel hungry.' Hilda and Bonnie look at each other knowingly. They both know that Annie gets crushes on attractive young women. Since her stroke of a few months ago her movement is curtailed; the object of her desires now are television personalities.

'Now to the business that we have all been waiting for.' Annie stands up. She takes down the portrait of her aunt and uncle and turns their faces to the wall. ehind the portrait are cellotaped three sheets of paper. She passes the relevant sheet to both women and says, 'Now write down your wishes for 2024.' There is a solemn silence.

'Remember be positive, keep your wishes to three.'

'Jesus, Mary and Holy Saint Joseph', Hilda exclaims, if any of my children knew I did this they'd have me certified.'

'You're not dead yet,' Annie projects.

'I'm ready' Bonnie says, very satisfied with herself.'

'O.K. Are we ready?' Annie takes charge of the situation. 'Who wants to read theirs out?'

'Sure I might as well go first', says Hilda. 'They're all nearly the same as last years. Number one. Lose weight and get more exercise. Well I didn't do too well there, I'm still the same two pence half penny. Number two. To learn how to please myself more. Number three to get away more often, while I still can.'

'You did very well Hilda, sure haven't you been away a lot this year?' Annie interjects.

'Yes, I suppose so, but not with people I like, it was like being back at school, being told where to go and at what time to go. I didn't enjoy a bit of it. I only went on those trips because the bridge club needed to make up the numbers.'

'There was no pleasure in it for you, Hilda?' Annie pronounced.

'Pleasure', repeats Bonnie, she plays around with the sound of the word on her scarlet lips. That is what it is all about, the pleasure principle.' 'Annie, you go next', prompts Bonnie.

'Mine haven't changed that much since last year. I'm still hosting my Sunday afternoons and inviting at different times the people I knew over the years that touched my life. Unlike Hilda, I know I'm not too mobile now so I can't travel but thank God I still have my marbles, I can travel in my head can't I? A girl can dream can't she?' She chuckles at her philosophical take on her situation.

'That's two wishes, what about your third?' Hilda asked. Annie rises in her seat. She drops her chin and takes a deep breath. 'I'm a little reluctant to verbalise my desire, as Bonnie would say. I don't feel confident about saying what my third wish is, not just yet anyway. I'll wait until you read out yours Bonnie.'

'Alright Annie, but there is no need to hold back with us. We three have kept our wishes a secret since the beginning. 'Read out yours Bonnie', Annie is eager to hear all.

'I have progressed a little since last year. My number one last year was like Hilda's. Health and Fitness. I give thanks to my tennis partners for that. My second one was Joy in my life.'

'Mother of God' says Hilda 'How do you parse that one?'

'SEX, Hilda. 'PLEASURE, DESIRE', call it what you like, that act of...' She stops in mid-sentence. 'Oh I don't know what I'm talking about.'

There is silence, the room is frozen in time, it is like as if the clock has stopped ticking.

'It goes on until the grave.' 'What does?' Hilda asks beseechingly. Her eyes light up, it is as if Bonnie is holding the secret to the meaning of her life.

'Desire Hilda', Bonnie says. She again plays with the sound of the word. She opens her mouth as if to taste the word.

'Let's face it where are we going to meet men at this stage of our lives?' I thought about it very seriously so I came up with the answer.

'Mother of God Bonnie, you're not serious, you have not', says Hilda.

'Yes, I have, the internet. I took ten years off my age and registered myself under the name of Babs.' The silence in the room now is not of lack of interest but of contained excitement.

'I'm Babs, a fifty-two year old active woman seeking suitable company.'

'Good on you Bonnie', Annie says, 'now please take us out of our misery and tell us all.'

'Well, I got four replies. One man was in his sixties, too old for me, another was in his late fifties, also too old. So I replied to the man in his late forties, forty-seven to be precise and I met him, we went to a lunch-time concert at the National Concert Hall.'

'Are you meeting him again?' Hilda asks breathlessly.

'Maybe I will, maybe I won't. He sort of left me a bit cold.'

'Men are messy.' Annie concludes that part of the conversation.

'Annie, we have yet to hear of your third wish. Come on, out with it', says Bonnie.

'Promise not to laugh', Annie says, 'I suppose since we are all being honest about our desires, I'd only be over the moon, in fact I'd pay money for Nigella Lawson to bring me breakfast in bed and then to join me under the duvet for a cup of tea. Now it's out, I've said it.'

'Hilda puts her hand on Annie's shoulder and says, 'We can arrange that, love.'

The wishes are made now and cellotaped on the back of Annie's aunt and uncle and the portrait is reinstated for another year. The business is completed and Bonnie and Hilda say their goodbyes and leave the apartment facing the dark of the night, like two book ends with the coming year's wishes between them.

As usual Annie pulls over a kitchen chair to the window to view her friends' final departure. She waves regally to them as their car drifts away out of sight. 'What a lovely night it is out there and what a lovely evening we had in here.' She looks up at the full moon through her dark glasses. 'How could anyone believe that there was a man in the moon?' She smiles. 'The moon is much more a feminine satellite. She searches the sky for stars but the moon is the centre of the constellation, the leading light. 'You will have to do Mrs. Moon.' She smiles again.

'Make our wishes come true.' She is back to earth now. 'Time to tidy up, wash the dishes and write up my diary.' She moves as if to walk to the trolley. Her little body crumbles to the floor. The pained cries alert a neighbour.

The following morning Annie wakes up in hospital. Both her wrists are broken.

'I'll have to feed you breakfast Annie', the young nurse's assistant says. Annie smiles at her. 'You're not Nigella, but you will do.'

A slow smile spread over Bonnie's face as the colour crept back into her tiny cheeks.

Éilís Ní Dhuibhne

Little Red

A thing Fiona does is online dating.

Not exactly dating. She hardly ever goes on an actual date. But she writes quite a lot of messages to people on a site called NEVER TOO LATE. Sometimes the messages are one line long. Sometimes they are just those little smiley things: emoticons. This is called 'a wave' on dating websites. Or maybe 'a wink?' She sends a lot of winks, because winking is a new experience for her; she has never winked in real life, with her actual eye, and doesn't know how to do it. It turns out that winking is one of the many actions which is easy to perform electronically but not in person.

This is how all that web winking started.

She was flying back to Dublin from a trade fair in Spain. This was maybe a year ago. It was May, but it had been cold, so she was dressed in her winter work n' travel clothes. Black with a splash. Black jacket, black trousers. Black boots. The splash is her bag, which is red.

As Fiona was making her way to a free seat in the waiting area, a woman doing the same thing dropped her glasses on the floor, and sighed. 'Feckit!' Fiona put down her stuff, picked up the glasses, and handed them to the woman. 'Thanks pet!'

She was large – the woman who said Feckit. Dressed in white trousers and pink flowery blouse. 'You're very good!' Fiona nodded. The woman sat down with a group of companions. Companions who were in good humour and expressed this with loud enthusiasm. Fiona sat as far away from them as she could, and buried her head in her book – which was not a real book but an e-book. 'I only use it when travelling,' Fiona lied to people – colleagues in the book trade whose lives were passionately devoted to the preservation of the traditional book in the face of competition from non-traditional books and all the innumerable other post-Gutenberg ways of disseminating stories and information. Everyone she knew believed that a book printed on paper and bound in paper or cardboard (not to mention leather) was a precious and beautiful thing, a sacred thing. They all had ebooks but only for travelling (to book fairs and writers' festivals, and of course ordinary holidays). Actually Fiona used hers all the time. 'It's just so handy!' But it has disadvantages. It's hard to 'bury your head' in a Kindle, and it doesn't send out the signal at which a real book is adept: 'Do not Disturb this Reader, who is lost in another world, buried in her book'.

She wasn't lost. Far from it. Keeping her eyes on the screen she eavesdropped eagerly on the woman talking to her friends, regaling them with stories. Cushy Butterfield, Fiona named her, in the privacy of her own head. The name just popped in, from nowhere, it seemed, although she knows perfectly well that all names, all images, all ideas, actually come from somewhere, somewhere in the thorny forest of your past, in your personal flesh and blood computer, until out of the blue something hacks in and wakes them up.

Often in the waiting area of an airport, waiting for the flight to Dublin, Fiona's heart sank when she heard the voices of her compatriots. The voices of the Others – the foreigners – their accents, their languages, always sounded beautiful to her ears, light and magical like fairy music. All those delicious butterfly words that she didn't understand. By comparison, the familiar flat accents of Dublin fell like heavy rain pounding the dirty pavements on a dark November day , like the murky Liffey crawling through the sad quays of the scruffy city. For a while, for a while, her compatriots pulled her down, until she got used to them again, until the good humour, the slagging, the colorful phrases, cheered her up and made her feel at home.

But she didn't feel at home, as she sat in the airport, pretending to read an auto fiction novel by Rachel Cusk on her Kindle. And where did she feel at home? Where she had last felt at home was at home, in her house, with her husband. Unfortunately he was no longer at home. Not the house they had called home together for twenty-five years. He had fallen deeply, in love with someone he had met at a book fair in Slovenia five years ago. It was, he said, a love which couldn't be denied. So ridiculous, so bizarre, so unbelievable. The divorce, solid as granite, had come through earlier this year, five years after he moved to Trieste, where the other woman worked – she is Italian, her name is Lucia, she works in a bank (so what was she doing at the Book Fair? 'She's a reader,' he replied. 'You know, Fiona. A human being who actually reads fiction even though she doesn't write it or criticize it or teach it.' Or sell it, like Fiona. He forgot that. Anyway the implication was that Lucia was an exceedingly rare type of human being, worth abandoning your wife of thirty years for.)

On the plane Fiona found herself sitting right beside Cushy Butterfield. What are the chances of that?

Fiona had the aisle seat. Cushy Butterfield was in the middle, and a man – Cushy's husband, no doubt – was at the window.

At least I'm not in the middle, thought Fiona. She nodded to Cushy, in the interests of politeness, then pulled out her kindle and continued reading (Rachel Cusk, a sort of auto-fiction novel, the very latest fashion – hybrid car of the written word). She observes the clichéd rule: don't engage in conversation with a fellow passenger until twenty minutes before landing, and usually not then either. She was aware that she missed many good biographical stories but she didn't want to pay the price of those – which could be, hearing uninteresting stories for hours, and being expected to offer her own in exchange. Fiona couldn't do that. She possesses stories – who does not? – but it goes against her nature to confide in strangers, and in most other people as well.

After an hour the crew came around with the food and drinks trolley. For something to do she ordered the snack pack – four ritz crackers and a piece of cheddar cheese – and a little bottle of wine.

Cushy Butterfield got four little bottles of wine, two for herself and two for her husband.

Fiona had never seen anyone doing that before. Most fliers didn't buy the wine at all, these days. They have a bottle of water, the bottle of water people carry with them everywhere, these days, rain or shine, in case they might get dehydrated as they go about their business and faint, or die. She felt more positiviely disposed towards Cushy. A woman who didn't mind passing the time on the plane with a drink, or being mildly outrageous.

'Sláinte!' Fiona raised her plastic glass to her.

'Sláinte!' Cushy raised hers.

The husband was snoring gently in his cubbyhole by the window.

'I'm Molly,' Cushy said.

Fiona introduced herself.

'Were you on holidays?'

Fiona told her she had been on a work trip. She never liked to tell people what she actually worked at – publishing sounded too exotic, too rarified, for people not involved in books. 'I work in retail,' she added. Most people were content to leave it at that but Cushy was persistent. 'In pharmaceuticals,' Fiona said, because that usually stopped further questioning (unlike 'in clothin' or 'in furniture'). 'Oh, interesting,' said Cushy, who herself was a teacher, retired. She had been on a holiday with a group, with the Grey Explorers. They had a great time. She gave the name of the resort where they'd been based, in a nice hotel where the food was OK but the swimming pool absolutely fantastic.

When Cushy was starting the second bottle of wine, Fiona told her a bit about herself. (Divorced. Two children, adult. Two grandchildren. Recently moved house to the country, on a whim.) She had also finished her first bottle of red.

'Get yourself another,' said Cushy. 'There isn't much in these little bottles.'

Fiona had never rung the bell in a plane before, for anything, even though she flies several times a year. But she rang it and got a second little bottle of red.

Cushy told her about a friend of hers, who was a widow. (That's not the same thing, Fiona thought but did not say. Being divorced is different. Being divorced is worse.) But she – the widow – met a member of the trouser brigade on one of the Grey Explorer holidays last year. 'And now they're living together!'

Yeah, yeah, yeah.

'It's time for you to meet somebody,' she went on. 'That's if you're still interested in the trouser brigade.'

Fiona said: 'I'm sixty-four.'

'Never use the 'a' word,' Cushy wagged her finger at her. A? Age.

'Forget it. You're a beautiful woman.'

Some lies are good to hear.

'And he's not going to come knocking on your door and ask you for a date.'

'What do you recommend?'

The Grey Explorers. Or... one of those online things.

The very next day, as soon as she got up, and before she had unpacked, Fiona signed up for a dating agency. Never Too Late, specializing in introducing people of a certain age to other people of a certain age. She provided a potted biography, answered a questionnaire about her job, hobbies, age, religion, what she was looking for in a relationship. Set up a standing order: twenty Euro a month, for six months, after which you could cancel it at any time.

That was over three months ago.

She has talked to various men on the phone, and has gone out for a drink, for dinner and once to a film, with three of them. The one she felt she got on best with dropped her politely after two dates. She dropped another quite promising candidate after just one meeting and many phone calls. It's easy to let these fizzle out – it is so common that the word for it quickly became part of the English language.

It did seem that most of those she met or talked to wanted more than she did. They wanted someone to replace the wife they had lost , mainly thanks to divorce, sometimes due to death. Someone to go to bed with. Without much delay. That they kissed – however chastely – on the first encounter alarmed her (not in a serious way; they weren't dangerous, or offensive. She just wasn't used to hugging and kissing people she had known for about half an hour. That sort of thing had been considerably slower in the 1970s, when she had last been dating.)

She was quick enough to figure out what she wanted. Less. Someone to meet for dinner from time to time. Someone to go to the movies with, or maybe even on holiday. Ideally, someone who looked presentable when out in a restaurant and could fix a blocked drain or hang up pictures when at home. Bed? That would have to be part of the deal, obviously – there has to be a pay off for getting your gutters cleaned. But the thought of going to bed with anyone made her squirm. It's one thing when you're twenty or thirty. Forty. But sixty? Seventy? She thinks her body looks OK – although the varicose veins, the fungal toenails, are best kept hidden from view, and generally are. She can hardly have sex, though, without taking her socks off. That's before she starts considering them. The grey haired men with wrinkled faces and expectant smiles. What does the elderly trouser brigade hide in its trousers?

Does she want to find out?

Caucasian. Christian. Leaving Cert. 5'9".

Likes: going to the cinema, music, walking.

Invariably what they are most grateful for is their families, and what they are most passionate about is sport.

Mostly what they desire in a relationship is a warmth, affection and a sense of humour.

Quite a few of them tick 'maybe in the future' beside the little pram symbol (which means 'Do you want to have children?') This is surprising, given that they are to a man aged between 63 and 72, the age group Fiona ticked when she registered.

The site gave them marks for suitability – good matches. The marks ranged from 70 upwards. Fiona thought 85 or so – an A when she did the Leaving – must be good, although it wasn't always clear why (Passionate about: rugby). Then she noticed a few which were graded at 125 or 130. Off the scale. Talk about grade inflation.(Where did it stop? 200? 1000? But then, why should there be a limit? Who's setting the rules for the dating site grades?)

A little simple comparative analysis revealed that what the men with these Nobel Prize marks had in common with each other and with her was that they were atheists. So that was how the website was evaluating matches. Not on looks, interests, incomes, favourite colours. Smoking and drinking. Religion or lack of it was the key factor, the thing that would unite you with your soul mate. And, when you think about it, that made a certain amount of sense. Although souls, hers or theirs, was the last thing on their minds.

*

On a rainy autumn morning she sends one of the atheists a message. *Let's meet for a coffee sometime.*

When theres a pause in the rain around lunchtime she plants daffodils in her garden – it's more of a field than a garden, a big patch of tough grass surrounded by a hedge of fuschia and bramble. In the distance the Irish Sea spreads itself out, neat as bolt of silk, although today it's just a sulky charcoal scratch on the horizon; to the left is an oak wood, the massive trees quitely shedding their mysterious druidic leaves. Early afternoon but the sky is darkening, and a sombre silence paralyses the landscape – even the sheep have paused their bleeting. There's stripe of peachy light over the wood and an eerie calm prevails, that sense of a vacuum, or the world at a standstill, which often presages a storm.

She comes in before the rain starts, and sits on her favourite chair, under the lamp, beside the fire, hugging a cup of coffee. The fire is not lit and neither is the lamp. Her laptop is closed. She just stares out the window, hardly even thinking. She finds she can sit and stare for quite long times, here, without being bored.

Sitting and staring is a thing older people can do, a talent they have acquired, somehow, without even working at it. You wouldn't call it mindfulness. Or laziness. She usen't to really understand with older people said 'I don't have the same energy any more.' But she's beginning to get it, the lack of restlessness, the muting of that urge to keep doing things. What is this life so full of care we have no time to stand and stare? No time to stand beneath the boughs and stare as long as sheep or cows? These lines have been in her head since she was about eight or nine. In the end, you get the time. You don't stop for it, but it stops for you.

She is staring at something, of course. Those ancient oak trees. The long grass – knapweed, thistles, Japenese knot. The sombre sea. The horizon... beyond, the coast of Wales, which you never see from here although it's not far away.

Sky ever changing, minute by minute it changes.

There's enough going on out there to keep her idle or busy, call it what you will, to keep her interested, sitting and staring, as long as a sheep or a cow.

*

Then.

A figure appears. A man. Outside the glass patio door.

He could be one of those guys who comes to give an estimate on painting the windows, or fixing the TV, or cleaning out the septic tank. It's Sunday, so that is unlikely, but here in the country they can ignore city patterns, they can drop by when they have a minute, then they feel like it.

This man is tall, with a long pointy face, a crest of grey hair springing back from his forehead, a touch of red in the hair still, and a sunburnt complexion. Neat clothes, jeans and a pale grey shirt, a grey anorak.

He smiles a snarly smile, and knocks on the glass. She has no choice but to open the patio door.

His eyes are grey like his clothes, and he fixes her with a steady gaze.

'I'm Declan.'

Is that Declan the plumber or Declan the electricin or Declan the serial killer?

'I chatted to you on Never Too Late.'

That dating website.

'Chat' on the website doesn't mean talk, on the phone or in person. It means sending written messages.

'Right, yeah.'

'I bet you're wondering how I got your address?'

There are no addresses or even second names on the website. Or phone numbers, until you get in touch with someone on the site and agree to exchange contact details. Some members use false names, and don't even put up a photo

'A little bit of detective work.' He has a grin which under different circumstances she would have described as attractive.

His accent is vaguely local – that Wicklow accent which is a bit like Dublin but slower, flatter. She doesn't remember sending a smile or a message to anyone from around here. But of course she doesn't really know where they come from.

Without being invited, he has edged himself inside, just inside the glass door. She considers leaving it open. Even if she did would she be able to make a successful dash for it if he tried anything? There are two houses nearby but nobody is in them, at the moment. People come at the weekend, sometimes. Not this weekend.

Then she remembers the other door, which he possibly hasn't seen – the back door. She could go to the bathroom, out there at the back, and escape through that door. If she could somehow get the car key without him noticing she could be gone before he'd realize it. That is, if he hasn't blocked the gateway with his car – the men who came to fix things usually do that, marking her territory as their territory, as it were. It is a thing she'd noticed, and sometimes wondered about.

'Aren't you going to ask me to sit down?'

'We could almost sit outside.'

Easier to escape, if they are outside.

'Nah. The storm is about to whip up,' he closes the door behind him and sits on the sofa.

'So, how *did* you find out where I live?'

'I found you on Facebook.'

But that doesn't give my address?

The grin again.

'There are lots of photos of the landscape. And of the house. The name of your house is on Facebook; there's a photo of the gate.'

'Rosamund's Bower.' A name Fiona had found in a biography of some Irish writer of fairytales who lived in St John's Wood in the early nineteenth century. She happened to be reading it when she bought this house. One of the first things she did when she moved was order a nameplate from the hardware store and get her son to fasten it to the gatepost.

Rosamund's Bower. A fancy, ridiculous name. She thought she deserved one crazy thing (in addition to the crazy act of moving house when she was already a granny).

'Then I asked somebody I saw on the road. Where's Rosamund's Bower?'

The friendly locals. As dangerous as Facebook, with their helpful ways.

'Would you like something to drink? A cup of tea?'

'I'd like a glass of wine, if you have any.'

'Sure.'

Isn't he driving? Probably not a man who pays much attention to the law.

Her house, this new house of hers, is open plan. The kitchen is at the other side of the living room, separated only by a low island. He can see her every move.

Unless she can manage to go to the bathroom, she can't get away from him – to phone someone, to text someone, to phone the police.

The police! In the town, fifteen kilometres away.

She goes down to the kitchen and takes two wine glasses from a cupboard.

'Red or white?'

He wants red.

'Is there anything to eat? I wouldn't say no to a sandwich.'

'All right.'

She goes to the fridge and has a look. There's some cold ham, cheddar cheese. The remains of a stuffed roast chicken. Bread which she baked three days ago.

'There isn't a lot.'

'You live alone? Nobody visiting?'

'No.'

What a stupid answer! She tries to backtrack.

'Well... My family may come, they often do, on Sundays. And you know how it is, around here. People are always dropping in.'

Nobody has ever dropped in the two years she's been here. Her son and his family come once a month, tops.

As she tells the lie, she sees her mobile phone, lying on the draining board. For once her bad habit of leaving things in the wrong places has paid dividends. And luck is with her. He takes his eye off her for a second, goes to the window to look out, so she manages to grab the phone and stick it in the pocket of her jeans.

He turns to look at her. She looks at her hands and sort of shakes them in the air.

'I should wash my hands before I start making sandwiches! I've been gardening, they're filthy.'

She'd normally wash them at the sink. There's a bar of soap, and a towel hanging beside the tea towels.

'Gardening in the rain?'

'It wasn't raining, then.'

'What did you sow?'

'Bulbs. Daffodils for the spring. And some crocuses.'

'Nice!' He smiles. He is quite good-looking, for his age, which must be somewhere between 63 and 72, unless he lies about his age on 'Never Too Late', 'Nothing like the first crocus of spring.'

'The bathroom's just here. I won't be a minute.'

He doesn't try to stop her.

In the little hall, she quietly opens the back door. Yes, his car is parked right in front of the gateway, blocking her car. If she left, she'd have to make a run for it. But she could do that. She could leave and make her way down to the nearest inhabited house, which is about a ten minute walk. She could hide in the ditch when he came running, or driving, after her – it would take him a few minutes, at least, to notice she'd vamoosed. The road is lined with thick bushes, brambles, fuchsia, Japanese knot.

'So you have a door here too?'

He's right behind her, in the little dark hall.

'Yes.' She is trembling now. Why hadn't she just bolted straight away?

Instead of standing there thinking. Hesitating.

'This is actually the main door, even though it seems to be at the back.' She's gabbling on. 'There used to be a bell but it hasn't worked since I... for ages.'

'You could get a knocker.'

Actually. That's not a bad idea.

'I could put it on for you.'

'Could you?'

'Sure. It's easy, easier than hunting down an electrician to fix that bell. You get a nice old fashioned knocker next time you're in town and call me and I'll come and stick it on.'

'The light there in the porch is gone too. That one.'

She points at the lamp, attached to the wall.

'It may be just the bulb. I'll take a look later.'

Maybe he is not a serial killer?

She shuts the door and indicates the bathroom.

'I'll be out in a second.'

In the mirror, she sees herself. Her hair with grey streaks – she hasn't been to the hairdressers for a month, she has been considering letting it go grey, or white, or whatever colour it really is under its many coats of fading dye. Her face is unmade up, and she's wearing an old blue jumper over a t-shirt and jeans.

When she went on dates with other men from the website, she dressed – not too up, not too down. She made herself up carefully, and made sure her hair was properly coloured. She had experienced the nervous preparing – the washing, the painting, the selection of just the right outfit – that she used to experience when she was a girl, getting ready to go out on a date with someone she was madly in love with, whose admiration and approval, whose love and adoration, she longed for. In years and years of marriage she had forgotten that feeling.

The pleasant tension, as she tried one garment after another. Not that she hadn't dressed up and done her hair and make-up, tried to look her best. But there was nothing at stake, unless you counted the admiration of friends, the eternal competition between the women, in the looks department. 'She's looking great!' 'She's lost a bit of weight!' 'What a fabulous frock!' That was something you could take or leave; it was nice, but it was like a predictable pointless gift. Like a scented candle, or a bunch of chrysanthemums. Not like First Class Honours or the Lottery. So the excitement of the challenge she had felt before those few dates with unknown men had come as a real surprise. She doubted if she could ever fall in love with any of those men. And yet, their endorsement, their approval, mattered.

She texts a friend. In Dublin. From the bathroom.

'I have had a visit from a strange man. He's probably OK but ring me in an hour. If you don't get an answer call the police.'

In an hour? By then she could be a corpse in the boot of his car (it's big, a four wheel drive.)

Then she washes her hands, brushes her hair, and puts on foundation, lipstick, and eyebrow pencil – in two minutes flat.

He is sitting on her chair, under the lamp, sipping his wine and gazing out at the field, when she returns. She puts all the food on the table. The roast chicken and the cooked ham and the cheese. The bread and coleslaw and butter. The bottle of wine.

'Let's eat.'

'Thank you; it looks delicious! Maybe we can go for a walk afterwards, if the weather changes again.'

'Sounds like a plan,' she smiles.

Her grandchildren visited her here, for a long weekend, with their parents of course, about a month ago. It had been ages since their last visit and Fiona was delighted that they had come. She did everything to make it a memorable adventure – got new toys, hid a big leprechaun (plastic, hideous) in the long grass. Made good food and brought them on picnics.

Told stories.

Since the eldest, Ellie, was six months old, Fiona had been telling her the story of Red Riding Hood, and many others. Fiona always told the traditional story which ends with the wolf being slit open by the woodcutter, and the granny climbing out of his stomach. But this time, Ellie wanted a different version. (She used the word 'version'.) 'Tell me the version that's not scary,' she said.

'What happens in that?' Fiona asked.

'The wolf doesn't eat the grandmother.'

So Fiona told her. At the end of the tale, the wolf and the grandmother and Red Riding Hood all sat down at the kitchen table and ate the stuff from the basket.

'Is that it?' Fiona asked, when she'd finished.

What was the point? Where was the story? And who had put such ideas into Ellie's head?

That's what Fiona thought, about the sanitised story. What she thought was, it is not a proper story.

No tension. No fear. No relief.

The key thing is missing.

But Ellie had nodded, apparently perfectly satisfied with what she had heard.

Versions of this story have appeared in *Little Red and Other Stories* (Belfast: Blackstaff Press, 2020) and *Selected Stories* (Belfast: Blackstaff Press, 2023)

Mary Morrissy

Remission

The treatment doesn't make me sick, it makes me dazed. And tired. Dog-tired. Fatigue strikes like a power cut and I have to sit down – now – or I think I'll die. The hospital is a stone's throw from Suesey Street, the part of town I used to frequent two decades ago, when we were an item. Last week, after my session, I found myself wandering there when I had one of my turns. It was a thundery kind of day; the sun was spiteful. There I was, passing 'our' pub. Where we would meet on days like this one, hot and humid, or on brown afternoons threatening rain, during our two seasons together. Either way, this was where we would meet in secret and hide from the prevailing climate of prying eyes.

As I halted in front of the pub, I wondered if I could still rightfully call it ours, since on the outside it had clearly been made over. The masonry is now a fuchsia red and there's a new name over the door – it's called Billy Pilgrim's. I suspected that inside would be similarly altered – primary colours, stainless steel, loud music, themed. Superstitiously, I've never gone back there. But needs must. Migrainous from the sun, I knew if I didn't take the weight off my feet soon, I would fall down on the street. I pushed through the pub's double doors with the same milky glass panels I remember from before, and became a visitor in my own past.

I made my way through the outer bar to our spot in the long back room, under the big station clock, so, you said, we wouldn't be reminded of how little time we had. The relief of sinking into pub leatherette was ecstatic. There was no one in the pub except for the bar-tender, a blocky, shaven-headed young man, with his sleeves rolled up and nothing to do. Apart from him the rest of the pub was unchanged. The same polished oak, marble-topped counter, partitions of dimpled glass, brass rail to lean your feet on, a snug in the front of the shop, a back room and a mirror behind the bar so that even before you've got drunk you're seeing double. The smell was just the same too. An oozing mix of stale porter and pungent urinal. I sat in our corner gratefully and ordered a mineral water. The electively bald barman landed the glass on the low table with a clink-clunk and obligingly opened the bottle and poured. I drank thirstily. The flinty taste of the carbonated water set my teeth on edge – funny aversions afflict you with chemo. I pushed the glass to one side where it spat effervescently still trying to be the life and soul of the party.

I confirmed the barman's suspicions that I was a mad old bat when I called him back and ordered coffee instead. It came in a thick cream catering cup, slopped obligingly in the saucer. It was thin and bad, from a jug stewed for hours on a hot plate of torture. But it was like a madeleine to our long-lost affair. With each sour sip, I was no longer visiting my past, I was right back in it.

This was the time of day we used to meet. It annoyed me that you would arrive breathlessly as if you were just managing to squeeze me in. But once you sat and calmed, we entered another time zone where all other pre-occupations fell away. So absorbed would we become that a parade of our nearest and dearest could have passed by and we wouldn't have noticed. This place absolved us from being furtive; it was the only time we were not mindful of our situation, where it became just the pair of us, alone in the world. Perhaps that's why it was so intense; for an hour-and-a-half twice a week we played ourselves. No wonder I hadn't wanted to come back. But as I sat there, I found myself soothed by the atmosphere, not haunted by the associated memories. In the torpor of an empty afternoon pub, I realised I'd found the perfect asylum for the chemically blasted.

It didn't stay empty for long, of course. Students started trickling in, a few pensioners arrived, men with caps and newspapers, and embroidered the bar. I ordered another coffee and settled in. Not out of nostalgia. I cannot be nostalgic for something I destroyed myself; I am not that perverse. I stayed because it was easier than going home. And then, coming up for five when I was totally off-guard, when I had made my own of the place, you arrived.

Really, it *was* you. You, as a boy, that is. Slender – you always said you'd been a beanpole in your youth – a thin hollowed-out face, gaunt almost, a mop of black curls and eyes to match. It was uncanny. The boy wore a sludge-coloured rain mac over a faded t-shirt, a pair of navy drainpipe jeans, dilapidated Beatle boots with pointed toes. If it wasn't you, this boy must have raided your youthful wardrobe. He sat in the outer bar in the corner but right in my line of vision. He – you, what pronoun to use? – nodded at the barman. He was a regular, it seemed. (Did you have a life in this bar before it became our haunt, I wondered? I'd never thought to ask.) He fished a paperback out of a canvas satchel and began to read. When the barman steered a pint towards him, he raised his eyes to say thanks and his gaze met mine. Well, I *was* staring. He raised the pint to his lips – I almost expected him to raise it in a toast – and then over a moustache of foam he smiled directly at me. Then I *knew*. Knew it was you, because that crease appeared between your eyebrows (the one I thought had come only in middle-age from too much worry) and your mouth turned downwards. You don't smile up like most people. It isn't, wasn't, a mirthless smile, just one tempered with a clownish sadness. I felt myself weaken all over again. Shyly, I smiled back. Why shyly? Because I felt all my old uncertainties return as if I too had been spun back in time. To a time before I met you. To a 'you' I'd never known. After the initial startlement, I felt invisible and pleasantly voyeuristic. I was happy to sit and watch you. After all these years, I finally had you all to myself.

Sharing. That's what usually dooms an illicit affair in the end. The mistress not wanting to share. But I didn't care about that. In truth, I didn't feel I was sharing you with anyone. She was just the silent partner as far as I was concerned. I just didn't want anything broken because of our association. I hated it when you talked about your past. Not because it contained her, but because it contained you. You blamed the past for our predicament. *Bad timing*, you would say. *If I'd met you when I was younger we could have...* We could have what? Obliterated your mistakes? Had children? When I still could. You could have brought out the maternal in me. *If you'd known me then you'd understand...*

Understand what, though? That you weren't always this rueful self? The trouble was I couldn't imagine you younger; I could only see you as you were. Acting old, your role to impart wisdom, already writing me out. *Don't do what I did*, you used to say, *don't marry for gratitude*. As if I were inundated with suitors seeking my hand. I was 37 and considered past it. Worse than past it, because I was engaged in a fantasy relationship that couldn't stand the light of day. That's what my girlfriends told me. Even if you had managed to leave the silent partner, I'd have got the worst of you, an old man enduring a guilty superannuation trying to win back his wounded off-spring. I would become the bath-chair pusher, the caretaker, witness to your decline. That was never my style.

For one thing, I've always been careless. Careless with people. Other people might mistake it for carefree; not the same thing at all. I am free of care because I care less. I was not vigilant enough even about myself, as it turned out. If I had, I might have noticed the giveaway pellet of hardness on the underside of my breast, right over my heart.

The clock struck six and a girl breezed in. She had long, sand-coloured hair and a gapped fringe. She wore something filmy and floral. Not your type at all, but then that's presuming I was your type. She looked like the kind of girl who'd stand on the shore with a towel to dry you off if you were in swimming. Girlie was territorial about you, fixed you with her big eyes and talked – a lot – some breathless account during which she would snatch your hand for emphasis, or poke you playfully on the arm.

'And then he asked me if I'd cover the late shift...' She exhaled indignation. 'I mean, really!'

You played with the ends of her hair and gazed at her with an unseemly kind of yearning that made me look away. Then you leaned in and kissed her. She was bruised into silence by your lips. That was something you used to do with me. In mid-flight I would find my words smothered by your mouth. It used to infuriate me that you couldn't bear my small talk. Looking at it now, I recognised desire. As you disengaged, another person joined you, a boy this time. I thought maybe I'd be able to identify him. Maybe he'd be someone who had survived into my time? But I couldn't. He had a face whose features seemed in untimely progression. He had a boy's eyes and soft chin, but a man's brow and nose. His mane of nondescript hair grazed his dejected-looking shoulders. I christened him Lionheart, but it was you, with your dark looks, that consumed my attention.

I kept you constantly in my sight-lines and every so often our eyes would meet and lock for a moment, though as the pub filled up with office workers, it was harder to maintain a clear line of vision. Girlie produced a phone and I could hear you planning the rest of your night. You wanted to go to a gig with a band called Methuselah, Girlie wanted to go for something to eat. Lionheart eyed Girlie, then you – he seemed to have the casting vote. I wasn't sure who he was most in love with, you or Girlie. Between the standing army of drinkers, I kept on catching your eye. A quizzical eye, at first, lightly sardonic, then more calculating, curious. This is how it was when we met.

I hadn't thought of you in years. Really! Not in that way, I mean. Not in the pained malignant way of the unrequited. But no, that's not true. I was requited. During that time with you I was more alive and more unhappy than I had ever been. Maybe the two go together. Now I am chronically content and half-dead. Though even at the time I knew what we were doing was a recipe for heartbreak – someone's. Yours, as it turned out.

In the end, I couldn't stand the tension of waiting to see who would break first. You? Me? Or the silent partner? I wasn't slave enough to the cliché to wait for you to say – I can't leave my wife. So I ended it. Chop chop. A swift guillotine. I remember your face when I said it – here on this very spot. Everything fell, as if I'd struck you. You started bargaining furiously.

'Here, I'll phone her,' you said, lifting the mobile like it was a brick with which you were going to smash your life to pieces. On my account. A gesture. Our gestures give us away. 'I'll do it, right now.'

'Put it away,' I said. 'It's over.'

It's not every day you get a chance to see the prequel to love. That's what kept me in a sticky, airless Friday night pub sipping cold coffee. I've never liked being alone in a pub – call me old-fashioned. Even when we were together, I hated being early. Waiting for someone I was never sure of, full of dread about being hit upon by amateur predators. That wasn't a problem now. If anyone was a predator in this situation it was me. But I couldn't bear to leave before you. It seemed important this time around that you leave me.

Finally at half seven, the three of you rose, gathering up your stuff and pushed out into the main thoroughfare of the pub. I felt the betraying heave of disappointment that goes with the beloved's withdrawal of presence. You turned to go; then you stopped and whispered in Girlie's ear. She looked back at you briefly then bounced towards the exit where Lionheart was waiting patiently. I could see his face lighting up as she approached. Ah, so it was her he was after. He pulled open the door and she darted through it. He followed her.

You turned towards me. I felt panicky but told myself to stop. I could see your head bobbing up and down as you weaved your way around the crowd that stood between us. I was trapped; this was too close for comfort. I had not banked on our worlds actually colliding like this.

Chemo fugue, my friends say. It was your ex-lover's son you saw. But no, I knew you had fathered only daughters. A trick of the mind, the light. But no, it was none of that.

'Do I know you?' he demanded.

When I didn't answer – well, how could I answer? – he rephrased it.

'Do you know me?'

He was more earnest than I expected. You were never earnest; had it beaten out of you, you said, in the rough justice of boarding school. You were playful in company, serious in bed.

'It's just that...' he started. A lighter voice than yours; age makes us growl and grate.

'Yes?' I said, feeling the bloom of ambiguous trepidation show on my face.

'Can I...?'

I nodded.

He folded himself on to the small stool opposite me that had remained empty except as a repository for bags and jackets. He laid these carefully on the banquette seat beside me. If it was a delaying tactic, it worked. What was he going to say? Could he do me for harassment? Young people are touchy about this sort of thing and I had not kept custody of the eyes, as we were instructed in convent school.

'You've been staring at me all night,' he said simply. No outlandish accusations, then.

'I'm sorry,' I said, rising to go. I had been a bad voyeur; I'd attracted attention by the focus of my own. 'I have to go...'

I tried to squeeze by him but he grabbed my arm.

'Why is that?' he demanded. 'What do you want?'

He gripped my wrist and looked up at me imploringly.

'Are you my mother?'

That broke the spell, the chemo fog.

'What? No!!'

'Are you my mother?' he repeated and stood up. There was the steel I knew from your eyes, the grit of refusal. I shook him off, my folly made manifest.

'My natural mother,' he hissed in my ear. When I tried to wriggle out of our awkward embrace he raised his voice. 'Are you the woman who gave me up? Who gave up on me? Who refused to meet me but feels free to spy on me? Are you?'

There was a ripple of anticipation in those around us; a pub crowd recognises when there is a row brewing. What I wanted to say was yes. Yes to everything. Except to the accusation of motherhood. To that I wanted to say – do you think, dear boy, that if I were your mother, I wouldn't rush bald-headed to claim you?

'Is it you?' he pleaded, 'come for me?'

Oh God, I couldn't bear the interrogative. I had come for you. But the wrong you. I yanked my hand away and ploughed my way through the crowds of drinkers, jogging elbows and upsetting drinks as I went. I stepped out into the laneway where more shirt-sleeved drinkers had spilled out into the golden evening. Once clear of them, I ran. I ran, clutching my false hair in case I should lose it too. In my haste I crashed into a stack of shopping trolleys parked in a bay outside one of those late-opening supermarkets. I ducked in and found myself in the refrigerated aisle.

He didn't follow me, or if he did, he didn't find me.

I counted it as a lucky escape, a remission of sorts.

First appeared in *The Irish Times*, 3rd August 2023

Mary Rafferty

When I am old

When I am old I will be unrepentant.
I would like to have more to be unrepentant about.
More transgressions.

Just now, because I have been good, I have few sins, public or secret.

When I was eight, I read my wonderful homework essay to the class. The teacher praised it. I don't forgive Bernadette Finucane, sitting behind me, for telling the teacher that my copybook was empty. But she did have lovely long, straight, blonde hair.

I told lies to my therapist.

I stole a golden, shiny powder compact from my aunt's bag, longing for a piece of her remote and impossible glamour.

I let my granny Rose think I was staying in the milk business, so she wouldn't be disappointed.

I hurt my friend on a beach in Greece, not being able to tolerate that fragile and extraordinary ecstasy.

I said words knowing I didn't believe them.

When I am old, I want to confuse the wild life I did not lead with the rich and small contentments of the life that happened.

The giddy laughter of endless nights fuelled by music and friends gets mixed up with the hot sunshine of the summer I left school, one kind of transcendence woven with the drunkenness of possibilities.

The thrill of flaunting my superior knowledge over that insufferable, gorgeous young man in college intertwined with the long months of care for my dying father, that closeness, dependence, and intimacy a precious gift.

The intensity of early love overlaid with custom, ceremony, ritual. The mysterious and dangerous merges with the familiar, intimate, mundane.

The energy of ambition is kneaded into the calm of mentoring, supporting, encouraging.

The investment in outcomes dissolves into the trust that it will all turn out, just not as I expect.

When I am old,
I will have enough, I will be enough, I will have had enough.

I will have enough, I will be enough, I will have had enough.
When I am as old as I am.

I will have enough, I will be enough, I will have had enough.
When I am.

Ailbhe Smyth

Unseen, Unheard, Untouched
A View from the Interior

Isolation is a continuing experience for me, so this is personal and raw.

ISOLATING

It's 93 days and counting since I've felt a hand in mine, at my back or on my shoulder. All that time without feeling warm breath, the smell of a small child's hot, damp skin, the embrace of someone I love, linking arms with a friend, the generous contiguity of the pre-pandemic world.

During the first weeks of confinement, I found myself wondering if for those of us who live alone, and we are many, (at least a quarter of over-65s live alone, rising sharply for those in their 80s and 90s) the absence of human touch is not the hardest deprivation of all. We are such tactile creatures. My friends said, isn't it great we have Zoom, what a difference the internet makes, we can meet for a chat. And we do.

But it's not the same.

Virtual touch is the ultimate oxymoron, leaving me with an ineffable longing, an ache, a need.

Sometimes, like a child, I pinch myself to prove I still feel something.

Mind you, it's better than the silent void to which 'the over-70s' in Ireland have been condemned. We are incommunicado. Over half of older adults in Ireland have never been online, a shocking lockout.

We are unseen, unheard, untouched. Untouchable?

Beneath the numbers lies an unfathomable depth of loneliness. Calls of distress to organisations for older people shoot up. Visits to nursing and care homes are forbidden. Grandparents are denied the joy and solace of their grandchildren. In hospitals, deathbed farewells are made via Facebook or Zoom. For a time, attendance at funeral services is prohibited and relatives stand in graveyards two metres apart as they bury their dead. The cruellest cut of all.

The full 'collateral' impact of Covid 19 on older people has not yet been measured, but the effects of isolation and the deprivation of touch have already been exposed starkly in the 'excess' rate of deaths of dementia sufferers in nursing and care homes. Loss of familiar routines, the stimuli of visits and activities, and above all the absence of physical tenderness are noted as contributory factors to these 'excess' deaths. Hugs it seems are necessary for life.

There is a great weight of sadness at the losses we have sustained which we haven't even begun to allow ourselves to acknowledge and experience.

'Children should be seen and not heard.' The admonition echoed throughout my childhood. I resented it, thought it was stupid (I was right), did everything I could to ignore it. Now here I am, officially old, silent once more. Plus ça change.

Isolation and confinement: two words guaranteed to strike fear in the hearts of most older people. Cut off from the most basic quotidian activities: shopping, going for a walk, greeting our neighbours, getting the bus. There is no law against these activities, but the tone of government 'advice' is severely monitory. You must... You must not... You will... Cowed into acquiescence, many older people believe they may be stopped by the Gardaí or fined for leaving their homes. Repeatedly I hear of people terrified to put so much as their nose outside their front door for fear of breaking the law and (therefore) catching 'the Covid'.

This is incarceration although we are guilty of no crime except to be our age. That's the problem. Being old is high risk, being very old is very high risk. Other people, especially children they said, are dangerous, potentially fatal. The world is your enemy. The only way we can protect you is to lock you up and pocket the key. For your own good.

We're not stupid. Older people are aware of the danger: a global fatality rate for the over 80s five times higher than the average; over 65s accounting for 90% of all Covid 19 deaths in Ireland (most, it should be said, with underlying medical conditions). We're not likely to be taking risks. But the thing is, from our perspective we're not the problem. You, out there looking in at us, are the problem. You out there may infect us. So we need you to respect our needs and refrain from engaging in risky behaviours that could endanger our lives. We know very well there's a balance to be achieved here, and everyone has to assume their responsibilities. For the good of all.

But there was to be no balance. In the early panic and chaos, we got locked up. They didn't call it that of course.

COCOONING

In the beginning was the word, and the word was 'cocooning'. Over 70s were to be wrapped in cotton wool, put into hibernation, minimally fed and watered and forgotten about for the duration. There would be no regard for the sharp inequalities and wide variations in the lives and circumstances of older people, just the same (what a surprise) as the deep rifts of inequality that mark all lives in our everyday world. There would be no need for any special financial or social care provision. Sure weren't we all safe in our own homes, didn't we all have the pension, weren't we all able to look after ourselves, whatever our levels of health, capacity, and fitness, and despite being cut off from the vital lifelines of our families, carers, and social networks.

After much palaver, the fuel allowance was extended eventually for those in receipt of the old age pension. That was it. We were on our own with our very real fears, our frustration, our loneliness, misery and deprivation. The world had far more important business to be getting on with. It would be very inconvenient to have to be looking after us, and to have us clogging up the hospitals. If that happened, difficult choices might have to be made.

They didn't think to consult us. NEPHET (the National Public Health Emergency Team) had no members aged over 70, nor from any of the organisations representing older people. Our views didn't count, our agency, dignity and autonomy didn't count. It was quick march, get them out of the way, stack them up where they can come to no harm, hugger mugger. And it will all be grand.

But it wasn't and it isn't.

Because when the chips are down, and this time, they were well and truly down, older people didn't count.

That patronising word 'cocooning' (perfectly described by our President as 'infantilising') tells a brutal truth about our society's ambivalent attitudes towards older age. We pay lip service to the venerable status, wisdom and experience of older people, but we don't want to be old and we don't want to be reminded that one day we will be. We are obsessed with youth, or more accurately with not ageing.

It is hard to see how such a society can not be ageist.

'Cocooning' was heedless of diverse and unequal health, material, social and relational circumstances. Our leaders were disinclined (or unable) to go beyond the dinosauric view of older people as frail, vulnerable and dependent. No one thought to query the rationale of lumping us all together in a 'one-size fits all' box. Why not lower (over 65) or higher (over 80)? Why assume that age is the sole determinant of inclusion in the box – not the existence of underlying medical conditions, not any of the multiple social, economic and other disadvantages which can intersect with age?

Ageing in the 21st century is a far more nuanced affair than it was for previous generations and we need to adjust our perception of the stages of ageing accordingly. Medical advances, better health care and education lead to increased longevity for an increasing number of people (although not all, which is sadly true). This means self-evidently that 70 isn't what it used to be, or 80. Or 90 for that matter. We live now in a world where the majority of people aged over 70 are and expect to be active, engaged, often working and healthy, well into their 80s and beyond.

And we do, actually, have views about our lives.

Nothing about us without us! I seem to have been shouting that about one issue and another all my adult life. And on it goes, without end. We have to resist!

CARING

There is any number of crises confronting – in fact already erupting – all around our post-pandemic world: from late consumer capitalism to racism, migration, and of course health, the economy and the future of our planet. One raised surprisingly rarely but of immense importance is the crisis of care.

As the corona virus cut swathes across the planet mowing down all in its indifferent wake, the response from country after country was to counter it with CARE. Because, for all our braggadoccio and rockets into space, we are not masters of the universe. Until we find a vaccine, the only weapon we have to slow it down if not to actually halt it is care. Care by, for and of people.

The countries best prepared for the pandemic seem to be those with strong public health systems and universal, free health care. Most countries, to different degrees, were not 'best prepared'. Including Ireland. It is thanks to the herculean efforts of dedicated health care and other essential workers that we have done better than might have been expected, although less well than we should.

Where Ireland failed catastrophically, although by no means uniquely, was in the protection of people in nursing and care homes and other congregated residential settings (including for example care facilities for people with disabilities; direct provision accommodation centres for asylum seekers and refugees, among others).

The majority of people in nursing and care homes are older adults, and the death rate in these settings has been horrific: 62% of Covid 19 deaths in Ireland are associated with care homes (reckoned to be the second highest rate in the world, although the rankings game is hazardous, I know).

The scandal is that for months there was effectively little or no protection for people living or working in these settings, despite the example of other countries, and the warnings, requests and pleas of nursing and care home management and care workers from the start.

The fact that 80% of these homes are privately owned may have been a contributory factor to the failure to support them. It may partly explain NEPHET and government oversight and inaction but it does not pardon it.

Fundamentally, this was a failure to recognise the extreme vulnerability to Covid 19 of the frailest people in our society. In the maelstrom of initial planning in early March, the needs of this significant group of older adults were not so much at the bottom of the pile, as simply not seen at all.

How this 'oversight' continued for so long can only be explained in terms of the abysmally low status of frail older people. They are among the most voiceless, and (living behind closed doors) the least visible members of our society. They were unseen, unheard, untouched – and too many died as a consequence.

That is a disgrace. It raises far-reaching questions about our attitudes to people in 'older' old age and indeed to all those who are frail, debilitated, or disabled. About how we shunt their care out of our homes, out of our sight, into places apart which one can only think of as 'dying houses'. This holds true for Ireland, the UK, and very many other countries. That doesn't make it any more acceptable.

One of the key lessons from the pandemic is surely that it is our collective responsibility to ensure that such a care-less and, bluntly, uncaring catastrophe will never happen again.

FRAMING

I was once in a photography class where one of our assignments was to make a family portrait, interpreting 'family' however we wished. I photographed myself sitting on a chair with a paper bag over my head, and called it 'Not in the Picture'. That was how I experienced my life as a lesbian at that time, many years ago.

That has changed in Ireland and I can now be out and proud of my sexuality. But the paper bag still applies to people in many contexts, including older adults. That makes me sad and also angry. We need to change that. We need, in the words of Prof Laura Carstersen, a 'new map of life' and we need it fast.

I notice I am often bone weary by the time evening comes. I think it's the effort of will needed to survive this solitary life, hermetically sealed off from the rest of the world; the energy required to resist invisibility, absence, isolation, silence, the sheer unendingness of it all. Sometimes, I shout out loud: I AM HERE, I EXIST, MY NAME IS AILBHE, and hope that someone will hear. I worry that I am on the road to madness. Because it's there, waiting for us, under the pandemic. You have to guard against that. And it's very hard to do without a helping hand.

CODA

As I review this in late June, restrictions have been considerably relaxed. There is now very little group-specific advice for those considered to be 'high risk' for Covid 19, including the over-70s, except that we should use our 'judgement' in deciding which activities we can now participate in. Effectively deprived of agency for almost three and a half months, it turns out that we can now re-activate this faculty. If it's still intact of course.

Here's hoping.

A previous version was published here: https://framingageing.ucd.ie/unseen-unheard-untouched-ailbhe-smyth/

Paula Meehan

Ends & Means

It is the old argument
In the *cafeneion*
Fuelled by *tsipuro*, fuelled by impotence,
Fuelled by despair.
I am weary of their armchair revolution
I am weary of their endless talk.
The generation of '68, the children of longing.

They are old now in the thermal springs
With the young hypochondriacs
The post-plague beau monde.
They sit in the pool the villagers have built of stone
To corral the boiling waters where they meet the Aegean Sea.
They are a privileged parliament, a hung jury.
They have come for a cure; they have come for redemption.

*

Last night I dreamt my children were young.
We walked hand in hand down the meadow
Then single file through the forest gathering mushrooms.
Deeper we went into the dappled light until
Off trail, stumbling over downed trees,
Snagged by undergrowth, sticky with pine resin,
Our clothes torn, our legs scratched, hair messed.

When we emerged into the clearing
My children's hands were become claws,
Their bodies furred, their mouths become snouts.
They faced me at the forest edge and snarled,
My little bears, they turned and left me
To waken, my cheeks wet with tears.

*

I carry my dream like a holy wound into the day.

The icon's finger points to her heart.

I light two candles for my two lost bears.

*

In the pool the bodies glisten —
Senescent, nubile, in the radionic waters.

This is an ancient *aesklepion*.
The sick slept in the sanctuary of the site
And waited for a dream.
The therapy
Depended on how the dream was read.

So the classical scholar tells me.

*

Off island, the forests burn, in Attica, in California, in Siberia,
The news a toxic fog.
The pastoral become radical again;
A poem about a tree to root us –
Blessed be bole, blessed be branch, blessed be leaf,
Blessed be all the tree shelters.

The blessed sequoias — great-grandmothers
Burning ring by ring: bell note of a thousand years
Tolling.

*

The salt water laps at the edge of the pool.
I am silent in the murmur of voices
The argument has moved on to civil wars.
How many generations for truth to be told?
I do not think there is time enough to heal.

The classical scholar talks of the Fates.
The three robed in white: Clotho, Lachesis, Atropos —
She who spins, she who measures, she who cuts.
It is all talk to me; all moon talk.

I think of my sister in the sweat-shop
Sixteen years old at her machine —
Her apprenticeship begun, her golden hair,
Her shining soul:
She cut the thread of her own life.

The heart wound too much for her.

*

The waves break on the pebbles,
Lace on the petticoat of the great mother.

I walk in sunlight along the ridge.
I pick hawthorn berries to make a tincture
To strengthen the heart.

Eight minutes for the sun's light to reach me.
Four million tons of matter into energy every second.

This I believe.

from *The Solace of Artemis*. (Dublin: Dedalus Press, 2023)

Caroline Moran

An Ode to Ageing

When I am old I aspire to be like my grandmother Bridie
with her *joie de vivre* and her kind ways.
I will read from morning until night, if I so wish,
I will rise when I choose and listen to beautiful music,
I will continue with my red wine habit
and on occasion drink pints of Guinness in the pub.

I will travel and have new adventures,
Husband wants us to spend a year travelling around France in a campervan,
it will be the making or the breaking of us.

When I am old I will set myself new challenges.
I will swim in the sea as often as I can,
take the ferryboat from Cleggan to Inish Bofin,
hang out with my adult children,
enjoy the company of friends.

I want to grow old.
My parents were robbed of this,
they both died at 65.
I want to grab as much as I can of this life.

When I am old I will love myself for who I am,
not try to change who I am,
finally accept myself for who I am.
Be happy to be me.

Teresa Mason

Letter to my 20-year-old self

Dear Teresa,

Don't worry, you will lose your virginity and there will be plenty of sex, mostly good, trust your gut about men, it serves you. The guy you still pine after was never for you, there was no amount of self-improvement that could change that. In the future women your age will not wait for a man to call on the shared phone in the hall. Worse than that they will be able build up an idea about him from what we call 'social media' and track his activity and on a handheld computer that doubles as a phone.

You might be on the wrong college course. You fail your final exams (no-one dies) and though you pass in the autumn you never really shake this confirmation of your status as not quite as good as expected. You will spend much of your adult life in education, possibly to compensate. Don't work in a hospital, it is not the place for you, you are better off in the community, helping people where they live. It doesn't have the status of the institution but it is more real, although you will be taken for granted, so are many good people, get over yourself.

Respect your parents, they are paying for your education. You don't need to let them know that you feel disappointed that they watch the lottery programme on the Friday nights when you return from Trinity College. They are good enough. Your brother and sisters grow in importance in your life as you age. You are very lucky there you just haven't realised it yet.

You will never own a home in Ranelagh. You won't believe this now, but you go back to where you are from to raise your children. The place also grew when you were away. It's what you can afford. However, the train service is excellent and this is just as well. Your batteries need the charge of the city. In your forties you develop a love for the rural landscape and an interest in history and old ruins. In all seriousness you do.

You do follow up your current curiosity about 'the root' causes of mental difficulties. You sit for eight years in a circle with a slowly changing group and all the givens in life are questioned. You learn and you unlearn. Each decade brings up an upheaval of this nature, when foundations rattle. It's the same for everybody I guess. You only learn about your own creative abilities when people mirror it back to you. Creativity is a resource for living, invest in playing, exploring and experimentation, it doesn't have to lead to anything to be important for you.

You will have a future as a blond. You will find that what you are wearing now is back in fashion in your fifties. Don't buy too many clothes, buy less but better. You won't listen to me, you will hoard. The planet is suffering.

Please stop smoking.

There's no right way to have a baby. You buy a lot of books about this, in fact you buy a book for every problem. You have an impressive library.

In the Ireland of the future gay people can marry. Women can now access abortions. They give out free condoms in college and Lidl provides free sanitary products. You will come to understand what Lidl is. A virus comes and ordinary life is affected for two years. We manage it but will be dealing with the consequences for a long time to come. An annihilating war is a strong possibility for your future. It again feels as much like a possibility as it did to you as a teenager.

Smash the patriarchy, it has a lot to answer for. At least start to observe how it operates and pitches you against other women. Remember too that power is played for by the woke. Woke means people who understand the right way to behave and think but this doesn't guarantee simple kindness and respect. Remember people generally do their best. Having said that Ireland is full of grubby secrets but the wrong-doings come out eventually. Many people are nursing wounds.

Teresa I'm aware now that I have been giving you the benefit of my advice and insights gained through experience. I hope that I'm not a disappointment to you. The advice will wash through you like water in a sieve, because no-one can tell you really and though you are pierced with anxiety and fiery desire you also think you know everything. Now you didn't think I was going to go soft on you and tell you you are great and have loads of potential did you? Do things. Think about things. Do things. A few good friends are enough, you will always find a few.

Much love

Teresa (aged 51)

Jessie Lendennie

Cotton: A Memory

I cried at the check-in at Shannon Airport,
turning my head at a memory
of my mother
in our old house on Highway 18
and the cotton fields like low clouds,
reaching the horizon.
I felt the sun again
and the loneliness of being
that comes when the sky has no limits.

But why draw the past?
You'll never finish the lines
and the colours will merge and fade.

Yet still the fields stand
and my mother works along the rows
and the sun burns down,
the memory fades with the heat
and turns to rain in my eyes.

Kerry Hardie

Tangled

i.m. my cousin, Rosaleen

How can I begin to unwind you
from out of my life which had bobbined
a shared wooden reel since our childhood

shone the damp mornings, the waves
that licked at our feet, the milk
from the banded jug?

Both of us, trapped inside matter,
joyous and sorrowful, amazed
at all the long life stretched before us—

till matter had hardened to hardship, but still
I could not want you released
into the marvellous light.

from *We Go On* (Bloodaxe Books, 2024)

Rose O'Driscoll

Driving to Mass

It was a very wet Sunday. Sunday in our house was solely centred on attending Mass. Nothing else mattered. Normally my father drove us to Mass. But on this Sunday my father was very ill with the flu. A most unusual occurrence in our house as my father was rarely, if ever ill.

My father was the only one with a driving licence in our home. My mother did not drive. Two of my siblings and I could drive. But we were all under the age of 12, hence we had no licences.

Despite this predicament my mother could not comprehend us not attending Sunday Mass. To do so would have made her the talk of the parish for the week. That was never going to be allowed to happen. My mother was a woman who lived her life keeping up appearances. And in a small rural community, that was paramount to your very existence. Throughout my childhood I felt my mother's actions and behaviours veered between pride and arrogance. But, of course you would certainly not say that to her face.

Anyhow, on that Sunday and despite my father's advice to remain at home, she rounded up all seven of us children. She told me I was going to be the driver that Sunday. I was 12 years old but I had been driving since I was 9. However, most of my driving up to that Sunday had been on back roads and country lanes. This would be my first journey driving on public main roads. It was also my first time driving with a car full of people. My usual journeys were with a couple of my sisters, never my brothers as they were always highly critical of my driving.

Our car, a very bright blue Austin A 40, registration number YZA 282 had a hatch back. So, with my mother in the passenger seat, four of my siblings in the back seat and two more in the boot hatch, we headed off to the local church, which was 2 miles away. One mile of which was on the main Skibbereen to Bantry road. A very busy road at all times but especially so on a Sunday before midday Mass.

The plan was to drive to the outskirts of the village, park in the local garage yard and walk through the village to the Church. Despite the heavy rain and knowing we were going to get wet, this was preferable to non-attendance at Mass. The whole plan worked a treat. With the car safely parked in the forecourt of the garage, facing outwards ready for the journey home, we made our way to Mass.

I don't remember the Mass or anything about it. I spent most of the hour and a half that Mass took being amazed and delighted that I had managed to accomplish the task of driving to Mass. This was such a great thing to happen to me. That day as a 12-year-old child, I felt I had finally come of age.

Moyra Donaldson

On Being Asked What Advice I'd Give My Younger Self

Dear younger self – sorry
but I've no advice to offer,
I'm still just muddling through,
no wiser than you and sure,
you wouldn't listen anyway,
never did –

that's not going to change
with a few words from this old biddy.

I can tell you there will be tears
and sorrows – but joys too – many,

though you will always want more.
You'll take your pleasure where you find it.

You will love and be loved
with everything that brings.

Your totem animal
will follow you down the years.

From here, I can tell you
you'll get through it all
one way or another;
smart, if never quite smart
enough.
You will be beset by doubt
always;

though the lies
you tell won't be found out – only
your heart will know the truth of it.

Máiríde Woods

Thoughts on Age from a Sixties Survivor

I wish I could agree with Elaine Feinstein about getting older and liking it –
though I welcome her call for celebration:

> 'The first surprise: I like it.
> Whatever happens now, some things
> that used to terrify me have not....'

('Getting Older' by Elaine Feinstein)

My feelings are mixed. The mundane looms larger: my body requires more
maintenance, boring tasks take longer: I miss objects in front of me and once
located, they often jump unbidden to the floor. Every little slip raises the
spectre of Alzheimer's – men in white coats taking me away. My children
never had to run away from anyone but one of them died young. I did lose
my only love. Some problems which I believed I could solve with patience
and effort have proved intractable. My enthusiasm for the new has abated,
particularly if it involves a password. Worst of all, the people I care about
disappear along with the fabric of my past. It is harder to sustain hope.

The curtailed future has changed my orientation – particularly in an age
of constant 'going forward' and religious doubt. All the positive thinking in
the world can't disguise the fact that in five years' time, if I'm here, I shan't
be in onwards and upwards mode. Even though I retain my Christian
beliefs, their absence for others limits the public consolation they provided
my grandmother. I hope for heaven but am unable to picture it, beyond
Julian of Norwich's words that all 'will be well'. Often the present, not the
past, seems like a foreign country. Perhaps that is how we are reconciled to
bowing out. *Ripeness is all*, Lear said.

I was born into a post-war world of scarcity – which leaves me impatient
with stuff. For my first three years we lived in North Wales, exiled by my
father's failure to find full-time employment in Ireland. Later we moved to
rural Northern Ireland – a place Dublin relatives called the 'Six Counties'.
So I was formed – and pulled in different directions – by both Britain and
Ireland. On the British side there was everyday life in the Welfare State, my
parents' attitudes – widened by emigration and devotion to BBC radio. On

the Irish side my Catholic education with its strong non-materialist and altruistic values – along with the spirit of resistance refined by a boarding-school experience. The wide curriculum and the critical approach required for A-Levels formed my intellectual perspective – no learned-off passages in our essays! Every summer my family spent a month with my grandmother in Dublin where the (relatively) bright lights, the bookshops – and the sense of Irishness – drew me towards UCD. I became one of those Northern students with a grant. (Thank you, Antrim County Council!) The beginning of the Troubles made me appreciate my life in the South.

So I count my blessings: to have escaped violence, to have lived in a country that during my lifetime has mostly known peace, the rule of law and prosperity. The abject poverty even a child would notice in the 1950s has gone. As a woman, I am thankful for the changes – medical and legal – which brought control of one's fertility. I also appreciate the equal right to work – though real power-sharing between the sexes is an unfinished project. I salute the greater official tolerance of minorities – despite a nastiness and lack of civility in social media. On a personal level, I have reasonable health and a secure income, though I quake to mention the former in case a new ache appears! Above everything else, I appreciate having grown up in a loving family. I had one of the best mothers imaginable – calm and a great reader; and my father, despite greater volatility, opened up wider worlds. I never listen to Beethoven or visit a foreign destination without thinking how Daddy would have loved this! I have come to appreciate the excellence of my education, the books and teachers who fired my imagination – as well as those who instilled some knowledge of subjects I hated! The lazy condemnation of all nuns is unjust to most of those who taught me. And there was little of the child-on-child nastiness I read of today.

One of the illusions of youth is to think you are different and individual even as you conform to the trends of your generation. My parents married late, I married early as did my friends. While my children were young, I worked only sporadically in the paid economy. I could have continued as a teacher; but I wanted to spend time with my children while they were small. I also wanted to write. It was then possible for a family to live – frugally – on one salary. However, there was difficulty in returning to the workforce. I served time in the *precariat* of writing, teaching and social research, before finding a permanent and pensionable job. And the kitchen frontline remained a constant. Now I'm glad of the variety of the jobs and the people I met through them. I greatly enjoyed being part of the paid work-force in the information and advocacy area, and would willingly have continued beyond 65. But I appreciate the freedom of retirement – particularly not having to commute. Being able to ignore job ads is another plus – I needn't pretend to be passionate about the latest career-fad. A pension in my own right allows me to live carefully. Occasionally, I feel a pang as one of life's phantom possibilities sails by, but only occasionally.

Appearance though is a problem for 'oldies'. Young people can look so beautiful, while all I can hope for is 'character' of countenance – and a touch of purple in my attire. The mirror brings repeated shocks. I may *think* I'm unchanged within, but the outer shell is crumbling. What's worse, my friends' are too. Now and then there's momentary non-recognition: *It can't be... yes it is!* I mourn the loss of 'all that needless beauty' I took for granted. And yet external decay brings a certain freedom to a woman. People who seek you out in old age tend to be true friends, rather than after something. One's relations with men become more straightforward. And there is no temptation to post selfies. I'm thankful to have grown up with minimal image consciousness. How can you get to know yourself in a world of externals?

I do struggle to reconcile the many changes – in myself and in society – I have lived through. Some things which were forbidden are now almost *de rigueur* – and vice versa. Some of the great leaps forward are welcome, others not. Perhaps we over-estimate the ability of a society to absorb change, and underestimate the underground nature of power. It's easy to crow about the demotion of the Catholic church, while ignoring the dangers of today's power-brokers: the capitalists, the State, the cultural enforcers. The insidious nature of media makes independence of thought difficult. Do I really think what I think, or have I been swayed by some influencer who has sized me up and argues that all *reasonable* people espouse this or that belief? I feel that the old Ireland – despite its limitations – had more going for it than the media allow. *Weren't you terribly oppressed,* people with a cartoon version of history sometimes ask? Sure, the poverty, intolerance, and denigration of women were dreadful, but there were good things too – security, some degree of idealism and service, flexibility in rules, individual kindness. As an old teacher warned us: *nothing is ever as good or bad as it is made out to be.* Misuse of power and exploitation of the weak have not vanished – new abuses and unforeseen consequences still sprout. However, being old leaves one freer to criticise the present – hopefully, without sounding too 'difficult!'

Age also brings a distrust of hype – I've seen a lot of causes come and go in bursts of hot air. Words of praise and condemnation have ballooned without matching deeds. I had a daughter with a disability and in the past campaigned for better rights and services for people with disabilities. Yet, despite rights rhetoric and solemn signing up to the UN Convention, gaps in support and services for people with significant disabilities remain. We get seduced by highfalutin words, without insisting on concrete improvements. I can't get excited about altering terminology – it seldom leads to change on the ground, and is dangerously close to pretence and virtue-signalling. Real change costs.

When I was young, music was our drug of choice and ours was the best! The words of that song, *All you need is love,* rang in our souls – we believed we could alter the realm of sexual relationships. Alas, we found conflict is unavoidable in human interaction. The loosening of sexual constraints does not seem to have led to better long-term relationships: the same problem of balancing self-fulfilment and attentiveness to another person's needs remains. When I read tales from the frontiers of sexual love and what is expected of women in a time of Facebook, I'm very glad to be out of it. Today's agony aunts still write of the entitled and uncommitted male – and Frankie Byrne's old advice: *Forget that boy* seems just as difficult for women to follow. Love is a hard illusion to banish.

Conversely, love's cousin, friendship, has brought me great support and satisfaction throughout my life – I remember the joy myself and my sisters felt when three girls in red coats came to stay near us! Different friends have taken me to spheres I might not have visited, while their warmth and sympathy have got me through bad times. Workmates and friends from groups with common interests such as writing, music, books, have sustained me in various ways. With other people a mutual sympathy allowed us to click from the start. When I meet old school-friends, our shared past meshes with our present lives. And I had the good fortune to have two sisters.

Nowadays the love of my children and grandchildren has become the bedrock of my life. My three surviving children live nearby and are a joy to me. They remind me of the existence of the unremarked goodness that survives the vagaries of the world. I am able to help with and watch at close hand their children – another generation discovering the world with that lovely mixture of curiosity and wonder, which I don't often find in myself. They distract me from the things I've lost, as a wayfarer over more than seventy years.

Moyra Donaldson

When I am old

I'll have dewlaps and a hump and say what all the time
in a cross voice: on every one of my bony crony fingers,
a ring. My lips painted with a slash of bright fuchsia,
I'll drink margaritas by the tumbler full and if my dealer
dies before I do, I'll just have to look for younger suppliers.
I can't imagine not being interested in sex, but if it happens,
so be it, really I could do with a rest, complete hormonelessness.
I may forget who I am and how to find my way home, but be
patient, remember I've always been more than a little confused
and never did have much of a sense of direction. If I'm completely
demented, I'm depending on friends: you know who you are.

from Moyra Donaldson, *The Horse's Nest* (Lagan Press, 2006)

Mary Rose Callaghan

See Lisbon and Die

A few years ago my sister Gay, my friend Éilís Ní Dhuibhne, and myself were on a return flight from the Canaries, en route for Dublin. We were over the Portuguese coast when the pilot announced. 'Good evening, ladies and gentlemen. We'll be landing at Lisbon Airport in 15 minutes. Please fasten your seat belts.'

There was a murmur along the rows. But everyone obeyed. The cabin crew sat in the emergency position near us at the top of the plane. We were flying Aer Lingus, but they blessed the planes so maybe we'd be okay?

'What's wrong?' I asked the air hostess.

'The hydraulics,' she said. 'It's an emergency landing.'

What the hell were hydraulics? Did that mean the wheels? Or maybe the brakes? Fifteen minutes passed. Then another fifteen. We seemed to be circling. But no one panicked as the plane droned on, without any attempt to descend. I quizzed the air hostess again.

'It's a problem with the undercarriage,' she said.

The wheels? But how could we land if they weren't working?

A man behind me panicked. 'We're food for the sharks!'

I turned my head, smiling nervously.

'You realise it's the Atlantic down there!' he said.

It had occurred to me.

Éilís sat across the aisle, calmly reading. 'It's an old plane. I know by the upholstery.'

I sat beside my sister but felt strangely resigned. My parents had had six children, three girls and three boys. I am the eldest girl and my sister is the youngest. I thought of my middle sister, at home in Ireland. What terrible news this would be for her. To lose two sisters in one go was surely excessive. How would she manage without us? One thought obsessed me: it would be far worse for her. And Éilís had an extended family at home too.

Gay woke up, yawning. 'Where are we?'

'Landing in Lisbon.'

'Oh . . . maybe we'll see it?'

'It's supposed to be a beautiful city,' I said.

Another half an hour passed and we were still circling. It's true your life flashes before you at the moment of death. What I didn't expect was my lack of fear. I must've been in my sixties at the time. I was in the youth of old age, so still felt young. That I would now never experience real old age was my thought that day. Growing up, I always thought twenty-six would be the most I could ever be. As years passed, this magic number got higher. A friend once reminded me I had told her I thought of myself as thirty-six. The thing is, you never change inside. In your mind and heart you are always the same person. Young people don't realise this, or how quickly life passes. Now that I *am* old, I still don't feel it. I don't know how this is. Maybe it's having no children? Maybe time stands still if you have no one to compare yourself with? I know wheels will fall off the wagon one day. I will get pains and aches and won't always be healthy, but for the moment I am. Age *is* just a number. Maybe I am a bit wiser now, but I still feel capable of making the same mistakes as when young.

When I was in boarding school, many years ago, my best friend was a pimply girl called Máire. We both hated games, so walked around the grounds together after tea, instead of playing hockey or netball. Máire was a brilliant student and told me all about Marxism and the Russian revolution. I learnt about proletariats and how all property is theft. This consoled me in a way as my family had come down in the world due to my father's illness. A few years later, when in UCD, I was recovering from a nervous breakdown due to his death, and struggled with philosophy. Máire was now an attractive young woman doing an honours degree. She came to my aid, giving me grinds and lending me a book on Natural Law which I still have. I remember one essay topic she set me. 'Morality is relative, not absolute' which formed my life-long thinking. Máire became a lecturer in Queens University but died of cancer in her early thirties. I often wonder what the world of philosophy lost when it lost her.

Another school friend, Aislinn, was a gifted musician and played the cello beautifully. She was a petite young woman who must have had feelings of mortality even then. She told me she'd become a Child of Mary so her name would be on a board. She turned up again when I was about thirty and we renewed our friendship, comparing the men in our lives. I was happily living in sin, but Aislinn had a penny-pinching boyfriend. She also died young of cancer. The death of these two friends reminds me to be grateful for being alive.

Old age beats the alternative – death. During the last few years, I read daily about people dying from Covid. They were all younger than me, which brought things home. Also, I often wonder how many times I've escaped an accident. I thought about this when I was learning to drive in my sixties. I finally got my driving test, passing out younger people that day. But, because I was older, my instructor expected me to fail. Despite politicians like President Biden, there is world-wide ageism, which didn't exist in Winston Churchill's day, or even Eamon de Valera's. It affects our own president, Michael D. Higgins, and percolates down to society in general. Many publishers and employers are ageist and are interested in the young only. Even if they are on your side, people want to define you, saying, 'You're marvellous for your age. Looking so well.' My friend, the writer Mervyn Wall, used to say, 'There are three ages. You're young, you're middle aged, and you're looking well.' People often ask me if I'm still writing, expecting me to be in a nursing home. I tell them Cervantes wrote *Don Quixote* on his deathbed.

The Aer Lingus plane landed to flashing lights that night. Fire engines and ambulances stood by for an emergency. My sister remembers the plane stopped dead and didn't scream up the runway as usual. It seemed like some giant pulley had stopped it. Maybe the problem wasn't the wheels after all? We were parked a long time on the runway, wondering what was happening next. Would we take off again for Dublin? Or stay the night in Lisbon? People were in shock, but there was no sign of us getting off the plane. At last orders came through and the plane-load of tired holiday makers hobbled off, some with walking sticks and crutches. The pilot bid us goodbye at the exit, looking spaced out. His voice was shaky.

'That was a great landing,' I said to the air hostess.

She nodded. 'It was quite serious, you know.'

The luggage retrieval was miles away and we waited a long time for our cases to appear on the carousel. Then we hauled them to a waiting bus. There was no help for older people or anyone. At the Holiday Inn we were allotted rooms after mothers with children were accommodated. My sister went straight to bed, but I followed people to the bar. I felt hysterical with happiness to be alive and, although I don't usually drink it, needed a beer to calm me down. Éilís had gone to her room but asked me to order her a glass of white wine.

The bar was closed but a waiter appeared from somewhere. When I gave my order, he said in broken English there was no white wine.

I was taken aback. 'But this is Lisbon!'

He shook his head. 'Wine not cool!'

'Could you put ice in it?'

There were no wine glasses either, so he poured half the bottle into a chalice filled with ice. Beer tankards were missing too, so I couldn't have a pint.

'I'll have two glasses,' I said.

No food was served, but there was great comradery among survivors. A white-haired fellow passenger and his girlfriend, insisted on giving me half a sandwich which they had managed to order. The tastiest thing I ever ate. I had joined my sister in our room and just fallen asleep when Éilís phoned. 'Wake up! We're getting a bus to the airport.'

It was still dark outside, but dawn broke as we drove through the sleeping city. We only glimpsed Lisbon's many beautiful buildings, but I vowed to return and see it properly someday. We didn't take off again till mid-morning, but were very glad to get home.

Meadhbh Ní Bhrádaigh

I am amazed

Coasting down the snow covered steep hill of our town
on home-made wooden slats called sleighs,
milk delivered daily from the
local farm in a milk-can.
Sneaking rides on the bicycles
of country folk
whilst they buried themselves in the secret
dimness
of the Alpha cinema.

I blobbed and blobbed
with pen and ink
before the biro gained its hold.
The annual dental visitor,
pulled our teeth in the school porch
and sent us back to class.

I had a father, a veteran
of the War of Independence
slow to voice the memories buried
in the corridors of his mind.

I listened hard but little was said.
Too late the questions now, unanswered,

I skimmed from
the best of times to the worst of times.
I am amazed at my artlessness
growing up lush and lively.

Becoming
all the time becoming
someone.

Áine Moynihan

Little Grandma

(Extract from a storytelling performance)

I'm a grandmother now and I think more and more about my own grandmothers, both of whom were huge influences and refuges for me as a young child. My sister and I called them Big Grandma and Little Grandma, as one was a bit taller than the other. Little Grandma was my mother's mother and lived next door. She was Annie Esmonde and came from South Wexford to marry my Grandad Dunbar who ran a business at the end of the street in Ferns where I grew up. They had a pub and shop and supplied all kinds of commodities to farmers of the area. My grandfather was invalided as a fairly young man and confined to a wheelchair so Little Grandma, who was sweet and gentle, worked very hard indeed to run the business and raise her family of four children, including my mother.

But busy as she was, she always had time for us.

She loved picnics by the sea, as did my mother. And an essential item for those picnics was a tartan rug. I don't have the original, but I do have the one my mother bought me just before I got married. (*Take tartan rug from chest, spread on floor and sit on it.*) I remember choosing it with her in Funges' drapery shop in Gorey, and I love these vibrant colours – colours of West Kerry in early autumn – the loosestrife and monbretia that line the roads. I'd been there a couple of times by then, as a student before my final exams and as a young actor on tour, so I like to think my choice of rug was unconsciously influenced by the wild flowers of Kerry that surround me now.

I do still have my grandmother's hairbrush. (*Take hairbrush from chest.*) A long time ago I wrote a poem in which Grandma's hair and that other, even older, tartan rug both feature:

From an Album

A black and white snapshot
falls from an album
there you are
tinted by memory

Fresh from your dip;
ring-a-ring-a-rosy,............................*(piano)*
first down in the sea
after seventy summers.

Your blue-green swimsuit
faded and worn,
you rise from the waves,
Aphrodite reborn.

A red tartan rug,
a hot cup to warm us,
then home in our chariot,
a blue Morris Minor.

A penny for a cotton ball,.................*(piano)*
A ha'penny for a needle...
You rhyme us, rock us,
wheedle us to sleep.

In my mid-life dreams
I still can see you,
releasing your bun,
gold-white hair gleaming.

Now I coil my own hair,
refuse to cut it,
reluctant to part
with childhood colour.

Your sea-blue eyes
stare back from my mirror,
fading gold hair
falls to my shoulders.

(more white than gold these days, I'm afraid!)

Auntie Nance

Now I want to tell you about Auntie Nance – do you remember? – my grandfather's second child whose mother died on her birth. There's a book or a show in Auntie Nance's story for sure, but for now I'll just talk about her love for clothes and her starring rôle in my life. She loved good tailoring and had the perfect figure for it – good shoulders, tapering down to narrow hips – whereas I tend to taper in the opposite direction! Auntie Nance had no children of her own but she delighted in her many nieces, dispensing all sorts of kindnesses and advice, especially in the realm of clothing. When I was a penniless student in UCD she gave me some of her lovely clothes. At sixteen or seventeen, I felt like a freak and longed for a pair of tattered levis as worn by the cool people! But they weren't so easy to come by. I had cousins with figures more in line with Auntie Nance's who looked great in her jackets, but she never gave up on me – right to the end!

Sadly, an amputation of one of her legs left her confined to a wheelchair for the last fifteen or so years of her life and she moved into a nursing home. Even her room there was decorated in her own style, with her pictures and small items of furniture from home.

Before her last illness she'd sit there like a queen, dressed to the nines, hair perfectly coiffed. I used to try to go to the hairdresser before I'd visit her as she liked my hair no longer than chin length. She'd turn in her grave if she could see me now!

During one of those long last days, when she really longed to die, she whispered to me to open her wardrobe, that she had put by a couple of 'little bits' (as she put it) for me there. I did as I was told (one did with Auntie Nance!) and there were two beautiful jackets, hanging together under a plastic cover. This is one of them. And I'm sure she wouldn't mind that now I usually wear it over jeans (whatever about the hair!) *(Take pink jacket from chest and put it on.)*

As well as clothes, Auntie Nance loved roses and she loved the radio. It was on the radio one night that she heard Nina Simone sing 'The Last Rose of Summer' and she was entranced by it. I managed to find her the CD and she played it over and over. It seemed to me, as she lay there dying, with her pink cheeks, as beautiful as ever, that she WAS 'The Last Rose of Summer'.

Kathryn Daily

Funny how grief

can burrow in deep down
like a worm, like a prickly sea urchin or some exotic parasite.
Lay its eggs, sow its seeds, deposit bulbs of sleeping sorrow
and then settle down to just wait you out.

At first, you think it's just the shock – numb brain mush
jumbled, misspelled, misplaced words and the world
disappearing as if down a tunnel, something to be seen
from a greater distance, from further back inside your head.

You swear it's just the shock as you skitter along
making the necessary preparations, the necessary old friend
phone calls, spend hours on the line with estranged relatives
who dominate your mourning with never before heard tales

about how their father abused them and their mother was unkind
to your grandmother. You think it must be the shock even though
you've expected this inevitable day since his first heart attack
when you were 17 sitting alone on the floor in a Vancouver, Washington

student apartment waiting for the long-distance call from your mother
pacing the floor of an Indianapolis ICU. It's so clearly the shock
as you and your sister giggle yourselves to tears before bed at the thought
of inheriting an ostrich farm in the middle of Nowhere, Texas

or as y'all with no adult supervision pick one of his punchlines
I know you did that! to be inscribed on the VA gravestone and lead
his only grandchild astray with a trio of hieroglyphic messages
for the genie of him in gold Sharpie scribbled on the bottom of his urn.

And partly of course, it *is* the shock, at least for a little while, for longer
than you'd expect, than might feel *normal*. But then it goes on and on
and on and still you don't feel anything different, no loss or absence –
the rumpled familiar love still tucked warmly away beneath your heart.

And then out of nowhere – maybe three or so years later –
a Friend posts a picture of bright tulips in rainbowed fields not too far
from his old house in La Conner, so much like the photos he emailed you
and the sorrowful seeds sprout in an instant, and grief

undeniably reveals itself in the tendrilling fullness of bitter bloom
as if you are watching a time-lapse nature documentary depicting
the raw ravages of surging climate change without even so much
as the soothing voice of Richard Attenborough.

Jessie Lendennie

What If

What if you got on a cross-country bus
And got off at the 10th stop
Where you knew no one
And no one was waiting for you

What if you had to live there
What if you couldn't go home
What if the bus home never stopped there again

Would you live the same life
Would you walk in the park
If there was a park

Would you have a dog

Would you walk without looking back
Would you gaze at the river
If there was a river

Would you fall in love

Would you watch the same sun rise and set
The same sun

Would you sit on the porch
Of the house made from dreams
Say 'Hello, Neighbour'
To the woman gardening next door

And when the onward bus stopped
Before heading out of town

Would you get on?

Sophia Hillan

Marianne Dancing

Recently, I have had much time to think, finding myself, with some surprise, in the days of ageing. In late October 2022 I woke up with an inexplicably fractured pelvis, and spent many months not only learning to walk again and regain my independence, but also to face the fact that, to echo Maurice Chevalier, I am not young any more. Unlike M. Chevalier, however, I am not glad about it. It's not that I want to be young again: I don't, but I'm not delighted to have to take fracture precautions from now on, and strong medication I have resisted for years. I'm not happy that, this article apart, I have felt unable to write a single word since the accident. What I am, however, pleasantly surprised at and most grateful for, is to have spent those months, between hospital and recuperation, in the company of some of the most wonderfully vital people I have ever known, some of them around ninety years old. I am discovering, through their experience and hard-earned wisdom, how to navigate this unknown territory. As Clive James remarks in his final poem, 'The River in the Sky': 'Simply because enforced/This pause is valuable'.[1]

This is not my first encounter with illness: I have written elsewhere about the experience of discovering I had a rare and at the time untreatable cancer at the age of twenty-five.[2] Nor is it my first encounter with age. Both parents lived to what was considered a good age, becoming, as the old people used to say of those approaching the end of life, more like themselves. Then, very recently, the youngest man I have ever known died, aged ninety-eight. In the Second World War, he was a navy flier; when I knew him, silver-haired, elegant as Fred Astaire, he used all his skill and knowledge as a geographer to pass on his enthusiasm for the wonders of the earth we inhabit. Just before his peaceful death, his last message to all his friends was that he had 'flown out'. When I look up at the sky, I almost see him, in his light aeroplane, skimming the clouds like his hero, Antoine de St Exupéry.

This unlooked-for sabbatical allowed me the space, at last, to read as I used to as a child, for the sheer joy of it. It meant, for example, that I had time to pick up and read (twice) Sheila Hancock's recent *Old Rage*,[3] her witty, biting, often furious diary-memoir of the years following Brexit and

---

[1] Clive James: *The River in the Sky* (London: Picador, 2018), 1.
[2] Sophia Hillan, 'Apostrophe,' in *Look! It's a Woman Writer: Irish Literary Feminisms, 1970-2020*, ed. Eilis Ní Dhuibhne (Dublin: Arlen House, 2022)
[3] Sheila Hancock, *Old Rage* (London: Bloomsbury, 2022)

the Covid shutdown as she experienced them, and Margaret Atwood's *Old Babes in the Wood*, the latest of her mordantly witty, unsparing insights into the process of ageing, not missing either its triumphs or indignities, or its inevitable catalogue of losses, great and small.[4] How could I not be encouraged by Sheila Hancock's account of training in her eighties, despite rheumatoid arthritis and incipient osteoporosis, to climb a mountain for a film she had undertaken to make, and then of making the film and climbing the mountain, despite the fact that, as she frankly admits, 'one night I did actually think I might die'.[5] How could I miss the truth of Margaret Atwood's observations on the necessity of all the tidying up and, even more difficult, clearing out that must be done when a loved one dies or when, because circumstance, accident or illness have left us damaged or diminished, we have to try to do it ourselves, to spare someone else the task. 'Others,' however, as Margaret Atwood calmly reminds us, 'have been through this particular time labyrinth before...'[6]

Yet, while such works do act as a memento mori — reminding me as I write this that I must reread Muriel Spark's deliciously unsettling novel of the same name — they also serve to remind me that it is possible to age with grace and dignity and, perhaps above all, with humour. So too do the writings of another woman, Marianne Knight, whose existence beyond a footnote in Austen biographies I came across some seventeen years ago, almost by accident. It was because of a small mistake in, yes, a footnote to an edition of *The Letters of Jane Austen*, mentioning in passing that one of Jane Austen's nieces married a Lord George Hill, of Gweedore in County Antrim. Though no geographer, I knew that Gweedore is in Donegal, not Antrim. I knew also from my own work that Lord George Hill was a pioneering landlord in mid-nineteenth century Gweedore: and so a quest began.[7] Nor was it one niece, I found, but two who married Lord George, the second after the untimely death in childbirth of the first, and that a third, the eldest of the three, Marianne, found herself in Donegal because she had nowhere else to go. In 1884, aged eighty-three, she left England for distant Donegal, where she was to stay for the rest of her life.

Blessed with a remarkable memory, and a capacity for both happiness and endurance, she retained almost until her death in 1895 not only the joy of being taken to the theatre for her twelfth birthday by her clever aunt Jane, but also the misery of sitting disconsolate outside a closed door while her aunt read

[4] Margaret Atwood, *Old Babes in the Wood: Stories* (London: Chatto & Windus, 2023)

[5] The film was *Edie*, directed by Simon Hunter, 2017.

[6] Margaret Atwood, *Old Babes in the Wood*, 252.

[7] Sophia Hillan, *May Lou and Cass: Jane Austen's Nieces in Ireland* (Belfast: Blackstaff Press, 2011), 37.

her latest novel to the older girls of the family. 'I and the younger ones used to hear peals of laughter through the door,' Marianne wrote years later, 'and thought it very hard that we should be shut out from what was so delightful'.

In a way, it was a powerful and prophetic metaphor for her life. Considered in her teens 'bewitching beautiful', she was known not only for her charm but also for her striking resemblance in manner and wit to her aunt Jane. 'Her greatest personal recommendation to me,' wrote her cousin Caroline Austen, 'is being very like poor Aunt Jane'.[8] Yet, she suddenly found herself one day in 1820, while still in her teens, excluded from the vital rite of passage every gentleman's daughter in Regency England had come to expect — her 'season', with its round of balls and chaperoned visits: in other words her chance of establishing herself in the only career then open to young gentlewomen, that of wife to a gentleman of means. She was brought up to expect such a life and should by rights have had it, especially as all other routes were denied to her as to other young women of her class. Yet, when her eldest sister Fanny, who had looked after her ten siblings since their mother's early death in 1808, accepted a proposal of marriage at the age of twenty-seven, Marianne found herself at nineteen housekeeper to her father and *de facto* mother to her younger siblings. Today, beside her fan and her gloves, her little white dancing slippers still sit pristine, delicate, in a glass case in the Jane Austen House Museum in Chawton, still waiting to be slipped onto the feet of a young girl, eager for her first ball. That joy was not to be Marianne's.

Even her consolation prize as *châtelaine* of her father's estate was taken away, as were her precious books when, some thirty years later, the estate fell to her eldest brother. No longer Miss Emma Woodhouse, 'handsome, clever and rich', Marianne became overnight poor Miss Bates, left with nothing but a small annuity through her mother's estate, shunted about from brother to brother as companion and housekeeper until there were no more brothers left. The only refuge then offered was with her last sister and a beloved niece, Cassandra Hill, in Ireland's distant North-West, Donegal, where today she still lies, beside her sister Louisa, in Tully graveyard near Ramelton.

A sad life? Anything but: Marianne became the whole family's beloved Aunt May, welcoming them wherever she was able to make a home, keeping up correspondence with those who wrote to her; yet always ready to pack up her bags again and move on. No-one heard her complain. Even leaving her beloved home at Godmersham, she appeared dry-eyed: 'She is much more cheerful than expected,' wrote one of her nieces. 'I believe she has cried out all

---

[8] Caroline Austen to James Edward Austen Leigh, quoted in Sophia Hillan, *May, Lou and Cass, Jane Austen's Nieces in Ireland* (Belfast: Blackstaff Press, 2011), 58.

the tears.'[9] Instead, Marianne wrote witty, light-hearted yet sharply perceptive letters, evidence if it were needed that she was Jane Austen's niece. When, in her nineties, her movements so restricted by arthritis that she could move about only in a basket chair, 'drawn by a capital donkey led by a famous boy', Marianne wrote that she would not be able to make the journey to a wedding of a young relative. 'It seems the fashion to be poor,' she wrote, 'so of course I am', adding, however, that if she could 'hunt up a new 6d' she would send it to him to buy a wedding present. 'If it never arrives,' she added, 'tell him I am probably frozen, or in prison.'[10] She may have learned to be at home in Donegal but, drily clear-eyed as ever in her nineties, she harboured no illusion about its drawbacks. That is not to say arthritis and the weather always held her back; another niece remembered her, a few years earlier when she was merely ninety, hitching up her skirts like a young girl, like Elizabeth Bennet, to hop over a stile, and avoiding the mud of the country lanes by skipping lightly from side to side like the nineteen-year-old she had once been: Marianne, dancing.

So much of her life was spent 'shut out from what was so delightful', but somehow she found it in herself to accept and deal with what she was given. Even in her very last letter, thanking her nephew Montagu Knight, the then owner of her father's estates, for sending her one of the treasures of his library, Jane Austen's own charade book, while it was clear that she had now forgotten her aunt was a famous writer, she found joy in the gift. 'I knew she was clever,' Marianne wrote, 'but in what way, I did not know'.[11]

Was it not, perhaps, merciful that all the misery of that early exclusion, and of exile from home and country, finally fell away? Is some forgetfulness at the end, without the loss of essential skills, always a grief, always a loss? Why not become like ourselves, all the pretending and striving stilled, the self stripped down to essentials, to the child who played and dreamed and thought the world full of wonder? Is it not what we do as writers, to try to get back to that essential self?

'What,' asks Carol Ann Duffy in her poem 'Snow', 'will you do now with the gift of your left life?'[12] If I can, I hope I may emulate Marianne Knight, finding a way to dance no matter what the circumstance, like the girl she had once been, like the wry, courageous woman she remained to the end.

[9] Caroline Cassandra Rice to Louisa Rice, 1853, quoted in Sophia Hillan, *May Lou and Cass: Jane Austen's Nieces in Ireland* (Belfast: Blackstaff Press, 2011), 151.

[10] Sophia Hillan, *May Lou and Cass: Jane Austen's Nieces in Ireland* (Belfast: Blackstaff Press, 2011), 219.

[11] Ibid. 221.

[12] Carol Ann Duffy, 'Snow', *The Bees* (London: Picador, 2011), 62

Lorna Shaughnessy

Lost Rites

Never again to wash your hair:
the ritual unpeeling of woollen vests,
my unshrinking shock at how thin
you had become beneath your clothes.

The dousing, shampooing and rinsing,
gloving up for the application of colour,
the – quick, quick – wrap-up and warm
your cooling head with the dryer

then back to the sink to rinse,
you spilling plastic curlers in your lap
and handing them up for me to fasten
with hairpins – always a few short.

Where do they get to anyway –
The same place as all the odd socks?

Your hair, like you, always bounced back –
restored to glossy, light brown waves.
Satisfied, you would nod to the mirror
and thank me with a small squeeze of the arm.

Liz McManus

Ageing

There is no question about it: time speeds up as we get older.

In the past I had all the time in the world to be a daughter, a sister, an architect, a mother, a public representative, a writer, a grandmother. When I was young, I lived in Canada, Switzerland, France, Dublin, Derry, Galway and county Wicklow. Now that I'm a septuagenarian great-grandmother there is never enough time to do the things I want to do. Thankfully, I am becoming more reflective about life. With hindsight, I can see my different experiences flow into one another. In life there are no neat compartments. We are the synthesis, it seems, of what we have been and the choices we have made.

At every stage in my life, I've read books voraciously. When I was a young student of architecture I read about the Greeks and Romans, Le Corbusier, Mies an de Rohe, about the mysteries of plumbing and the principles of structural engineering. Regrettably, despite my efforts, none of the books I read helped me to become a good architect. It wasn't the books' fault : my brain just couldn't fathom how electricity is made or the purpose of reinforced concrete. As architects go, I was an abject failure. For a few years after graduating, I managed to hide that fact long enough to work in architects' offices in Derry and Galway. During the recession of the 1980s, when the building trade was on its knees, I was glad to escape out of employment and into fulltime motherhood.

Caring for four small children kept me busy to the point of exhaustion but I never stopped reading. A plethora of books has been written about child-rearing and, sometimes it felt as if, as a young mother, I had read them all. My bible was Dr Spock's *Baby and Child Care*. Although he recanted on a few opinions in that book, I will be eternally grateful to Benjamin Spock for his reassurance to young mothers like me: 'You know more than you think you do...'

I kept reading and then I began to write. At first, I wrote a column in 'The Sunday Tribune' newspaper. When I began to write fiction I discovered that an endless number of books have been published about the art of writing. I must confess that most books I have read on the subject are ponderously written and even at times, self-serving. Stephen King's *On*

Writing is, to my mind, an honourable exception.

What is my point? You may well ask.

My point is that there are things that can't be learnt from books. One of them is how to be a parliamentarian. Looking back, I realise I've had long and varied political experience. For thirty-two years, I was an elected public representative: firstly, as a county councillor, then as a TD for nineteen years and then, a Minister of State for three years. During all that time, I never once read a book about how to become a good public representative. There are no books on the subject. None that I could find anyway.

The skills of public representation are learnt through day-to-day experience, usually the hard way by trial and error, or else, they are transmitted by word of mouth within the political community. As is often the case with Irish politics, that knowledge may be transmitted down through the generations within families. Dick Spring once said that, even though he became the General Election candidate after his father retired from Dáil Éireann, the people of Kerry were still voting at election time for his father, Dan Spring.

I came to politics from Left – literally – field. My father was a senior civil servant who had a disdain for all politicians. My mother was an artist with no political interest. Conversations at home were about everything except politics. I learnt my politics through campaigning in the streets. As a neophyte with no family connections in politics, I had to trust my instincts when it came to making my way through the arcane world of our democratic institutions. Any advice I received along the way was useful. On my first day in Leinster House I was struggling to find my feet – as well as figuring out the whereabouts of the ladies lavatory – when an older TD from county Clare, whom I didn't know, approached me and gripped my arm. To my surprise he growled, 'You're new. My advice is simple: keep away from the media. They are all animals.'

In the hothouse environment of Dáil Éireann I was aware that every TD is dependent on the media for exposure so his advice was not very practical. All the same, I discovered that the well-meaning TD had done me a favour. From then on, I was on my guard when being interviewed, which was no bad thing when enjoined in the battle of wits with the Fourth estate.

For any public representative, the most important guidance comes from the constituents themselves. Listening to peoples' stories, crises, conversations, confessions, and good counsel is part and parcel of a TDs work. Today there is a fashion for dismissing this aspect of public representation as mere clientelism but I consider it an invaluable resource for the work of a legislator. Even if, at times, the extent of the difficulties that people endure in their daily lives, can be overwhelming, a good TD needs to listen to them because the stories they tell often illuminate the deficiencies that need to be addressed.

Here is a simple example of what I mean. In 1992 I had stood as a candidate in the general election because I believed – and I still do – that women must be included in our parliament on the basis of equality. I'd been active in the women's movement for a long time before I came into Dáil Éireann. Side by side with other women, I had fought for contraception to be made widely available, for battered women to be protected, for equality for women under the law, for the right to serve of juries and the right to equal pay. The list goes on... Over the years, as each of these wrongs was being righted, I was confident that Ireland was becoming a better place for women and, by extension, for men too.

Pandora's box had been well and truly opened. In 1992, a large (compared to previous elections), and new cohort of women, including me, was elected to Dáil Éireann. President Mary Robinson was already installed in the Áras. They were heady times indeed.

A month after the election I started holding clinics around county Wicklow. An advertisement was placed in the local *Wicklow People* newspaper and I dutifully drove around the county in order to sit in draughty halls, or in rooms over pubs and wait for anyone who wanted to come in and talk to me. These were pre-mobile phones and pre-emails times so politics was close up and personal then. Men and women told me about their minor problems or their major crises. It is a unique relationship: because they vote, people feel ownership of their public representative. It is a meeting of equals.

At my first clinic in rural Wicklow a woman I had never met before, was waiting for me when I arrived. She sat down and told me that she had had a contraceptive coil fitted in the Well Woman Centre in Dublin and she wanted to know if she needed to have it checked. How long is it since you had it fitted or checked? I asked.

Fifteen years, was her answer.

Here was a woman who had nobody else to turn to. She couldn't go to her doctor (too religious) for a consultation. She couldn't go to her local family planning centre because there was none. Undaunted, she consulted her newbie female TD and went away, satisfied with the advice I gave her. But she gave me a valuable lesson too. Because of her, I understood that all the advances made by women had failed to reach all the women who needed them. Hers was only one of many stories that I heard during my years as a TD. All of them fed into my understanding of the meaning of public representation.

Life, according to the philosopher Kierkegaard can only be understood backwards but it must be lived forwards and yet, when I look back, as an older woman, all my life seems to have been in a state of flux. The Ireland I grew up in has been utterly transformed. Indeed, far from slowing down, the rate of change is speeding up. At times the challenges are disconcerting. To access your bank account these days requires you to have a diploma in IT and there is rarely, if ever, a human being to talk to when you phone up a company looking for help. The joke about the automated answering service: *Your call is important to us. Please hold on until it is no longer important to you* is not really a joke. It is life as we know it now.

Despite the development of AI, Kindle and the other technological advances, I take comfort in the fact that books are still being published. The public are reading books more than ever. I can understand why. Ancient people depended on storytelling to wrestle with their demons. For me, the same desire to understand life's mutability is always satisfied by reading between the covers of a book.

Kathryn Daily

How He Courted Me

He reached his hand out
towards my cheek
and gently with his eyes
touched the part of me
that age cannot.

Áine Ryan

Out there on the island

The best place to grow old is out there on the island. That is what I told the pirate princesses, my O'Malley daughters, when I was preoccupied by death because of Daddy's dementia.

When the time comes to put me 'out to grass', I said, despatch me back across the bay, out to the island, where I can wander the byways and boreens talking to myself. There, I can wear my red or pink beret and smoke Gitanes cigarettes, just like I did when I was a student in the hallowed halls of Maynooth.

I can wander down to the bar too, I told them, and order double whiskeys, take out my false teeth, put them in a pint glass and eat cheese and onion crisps without little slivers getting caught in the gaps between my molars. If I fancy too, I can sing Raglan Road as if I am Hilda, Paddy Kavanagh's muse, and, indeed, if there happens to be an ould seisiún unfolding, throw my walking stick aside and jump up for a half-set, dance a Shoe the Donkey.

If I feel like it too, I can flirt outrageously with the young island men who lean across high stools in oilskins and wellingtons and smell of sea salt and mackerel, or lobster. and crab claws.

Pirate Princesses

The princesses will roll their eyes up to heaven, of course. They will say: 'There she goes again.'

That is because the minutiae and realities of ageing are inevitably lost on the young, even the middle-aged, as life expectancy stretches out there across the horizon. On the one hand, the media monster is obsessed with stories and pictures of celebrities who have embraced cosmetic surgery. Red-carpet images of septuagenarians with plunging dresses showing off bolstered boobs which have been transformed into weapons of mass seduction are commonplace. Conversely these same media masters and mistresses define and debase ordinary old age with images of wrinkled hands and dandruff-flecked slippers.

Indeed, the societal realities of ageing only crystallised for me when I began writing a series with a working title of 'Daddy, Dementia and Me' for The Irish Times in 2018. It was about George's shenanigans during his final years. In desperation, we had uprooted him – without his permission – from Dublin to a nursing home in Westport, where my brother and I live. Living independently had become increasingly precarious due to Daddy's short-term memory loss. As the saying goes, he had become a danger to himself and, in one particular instance, to his neighbours.

This was due to his insistence on using his leftover chips to light his fire. An ingenious discovery, according to the incorrigible George. This had culminated in a little visit from the fire-brigade one balmy evening. Interestingly, his daily trip across to the chipper on Tyrconnell Road wasn't simply about purchasing his main meal of the day, which he argued, by the way, was full of nutrition since it also included a portion of deep-fried battered onions.

He was also teaching the Polish owner some choice Irish phrases such as Póg mo Thóin and other unmentionable diatribes.

Add in the rather unnerving fact that he insisted on withdrawing large amounts of cash from the bank – about €10,000 a go – wads of which he would haul out of his wallet whilst standing in the queue in the chipper.

Writing the series from an ironic and humourous perspective helped to salve my existential fears. It helped me to cope with the long goodbye of losing George – bit by bit, brain cell by brain cell.

Don't imagine for a minute, however, that there was anything predictable about this journey. Daddy didn't just fade away. He wasn't just neutralised by his incarceration in a nursing home. His bold boyish spirit prevailed until the end, even when it was numbed by drugs, slowed down by heart failure, compromised by creaking limbs.

Take his hilarious flirtation with one of his favourite carers: an amazing young woman, who managed him with the panache of an acrobat who happened to have eyelashes that fluttered like the prettiest butterfly.

'Áine,' he would say, with a wicked twinkle in his eye every time Karolina came into his room. 'Would you just look at her, Áine. Isn't she so beeauutt....iful.

'So, so beaut .....iful?'

This mantra was repeated on every occasion when Karolina came into his room when I was visiting him. Until, one day, another carer, whose eyelashes did not flutter quite like a butterfly's, came in to tell him it was teatime.

George was a little groggy having just awoken from a snore fest that would challenge the percussion section of a philharmonic orchestra.

Pulling himself up onto his pillow he declared, without looking up: 'Áine, oh Áine. Would you just look at her?'

But, as alertness returns, there is a sudden pause.

'Isn't she so ..... so ..... so inter......esting, Áine. So interesting.'

Byways and boreens

I have told my island-born daughters that when the time comes to put me 'out to grass' I will wander the byways and boreens through Faungloss and Capnagower, Ballytoughey Mór and Maum, gathering wild flowers to make garlands of daisies or bog cotton for my grey thinning hair. I will play hide-and-seek with the baby lambs and sit on hummocks of spongy peat out on the edge of the cliffs at Coinne Rón. Occasionally, I will allow myself slip back across the ocean to meet for secret trysts with old lovers. I will talk to them of could-have-beens and would-have-beens. Reach out into the warm south-westerly breeze and snatch a kiss, hold a hug deep into my heart, allow the scent of teenage innocence recapture my soul.

Bold boys and missing cars

When I arrive at the nursing home around my usual mid-afternoon time, Daddy is having yet another stand-off about his car. The car that was sold over three years ago. The last car in which he drove down the byways and boreens of Ireland covering bridge congresses for The Irish Times until 2014. The lovely staff have already brought him outside in search of the errant car. He claims it is just 'down there, through the gate and around the corner'.

We all know the only mobile entity down there is a sheep that is partial to the long acre. But George was in bold boy mode, quoting his rights under *Bunreacht na hÉireann* and cursing like a sailor.

'You don't have a car anymore, Daddy. It was sold three years ago because your short-term memory loss meant it was dangerous for you to drive.'

'Stop bullshitting me, Áine. Do you think I am some kind of a f***ing eejit?'

'Daddy, You know the way you always say that while you may have lost your short-term memory, you haven't lost your powers of reasoning, please listen to me.'

Not a chance. He is gone, striding down the corridor for his coat. If I won't help him find his car, he'll do it himself.

In the end, there is nothing for it but to put on his Columbo trench coat and cap, sign him out and go looking for the elusive car.

'Okay, let's go find it, daddy.'

His sense of relief is palpable, his confusion calmed, as my heart thumps in my throat.

After I strap him into the front seat of my car we head off on a most bizarre wild goose chase. He orders me not to take the usual bend back towards Westport but to drive straight on through a Bermuda triangle of narrow roads strewn with lumps of kelp that eventually bring us to the edge of Clew Bay.

'It is just around the next corner, Áine. No, maybe, it is the next one. I think it's black. Or was it blue? I just can't remember its registration.'

Thus our pilgrimage continued until we landed at the still waters of Westport Quay where the pyramidal peak of Croagh Patrick was clear and snowcapped.

'What mountain is that, Daddy?'

'It's a holy one, Áine.'

At last, we sit in silence lulled by the beauty of this natural amphitheatre.

'Will you recite me your favourite, poem, Daddy?'

> 'Up the airy mountain,
> Down the rushy glen,
> We daren't go a-hunting,
> For fear of little men.
> Wee folk, good folk,
> Trooping all together,
> Green jacket, red cap,
> And white owl's feather'.

(William Allingham)

The room above

Seven days after his 91st birthday, on November 9, 1992, my islander father-in-law, faded out of this world and, surrounded by three generations of his family. He was waked for two nights in 'the room above', in the bed he had shared with Katie Ann, his wife for over 60 years. His widow and youngest son helped 'put him over-board' – the expression still used on the island for laying out a corpse. They propped his chin in place with a hardback copy of Muiris Ó Súilleabháin's Blasket Island memoir, *Twenty Years A-Growing*, tied around his head with a teacloth.

Born in 1901, Austy Bob O'Malley had a long happy life: shoeing donkeys and horses in the little forge out in the yard; saving the hay with a scythe and cutting the turf with a sléan. He whistled the polkas and the reels for house dances and tapped the top off his daily boiled egg like a sculptor creating a great masterpiece.

Once dusk had crept in over the horizon in the evenings, he would sit in his chair on the left side of the range – herself on the other side – and fill his pipe with the concentration of a forensic scientist. This was his time for puffing plumes of smoke up over the Sacred Heart lamp while reading and snoozing. It could be Aleksandr Solzhenitsyn's *The Gulag Archipelago* or John B Keane's *Letters of a Love-Hungry Farmer*. He took the tales he read in every tome he devoured – whether fact or fiction – with a big pinch of salt peppered with a laugh which often involved the dislocation of his peaked cap from its perennial perch as he threw his head back and slapped his knees.

'I just want to be in my home.'

Minutes before Daddy died on April 21, 2020, I sang Raglan Road down the phone to him whilst snottering and bawling crying. It was during the Covid pandemic and I hadn't been able to visit him for weeks, due to the restrictions. On that last visit I had brought him a bunch of daffodils and a chocolate Easter bunny, which he decapitated with one gulp before taking a deep pull out of his cigarette. We were in his happy place, the smoking room.

George ended up here in the wild west because he had been expelled for a plethora of reasons from his first nursing home in Dublin. Unsurprisingly, the rebelliousness continued when we moved him to the Pilgrim's Rest in Westport in the spring of 2015.

He quickly became like a Houdini, secreting lighters or boxes of matches he had conjured from nowhere and, like the bold schoolboy he was, sneaking off to the loo for a smoke. Of course, the ingenious owners and staff were ever-vigilant. On one of these occasions when the wafts of nicotine were meandering down the corridor, Pauline Mulroy deliberately turned on the smoke alarm, waited a moment and then called out to him in an angelic voice.

'You'd never be in there having a cigarette now, George, would you?'

'Well, f**k it anyway,' was the retort from the loo.

Over the following months he tried every ruse and strategy to escape, to find that elusive car he no longer owned and drive back to his little apartment in Inchicore.

'I just want to be in my home, Áine,' he repeated, again and again. 'I just want to be in my home.'

Katie Donovan

Widow

I spend a lot of time
with a smile
stretched across the chasm
of my face;
like one of those outcast chimps
who grins too much –
teeth bared in a rictus
of placate.

from *Off Duty* (Bloodaxe Books, 2016)

Sheila Barrett

Limping to Byzantium

My brother-in-law says, 'Home is a time, not a place'. He has spent most of his life away from Ireland, just as I've spent most of mine away from America. I love these conversations, these remarks in passing. We sift memories now, while we try to tame our environments. What matters? What do we really need? At this stage of life, you'd want to travel as light as a marathon runner, the better to stay the course.

My home here in Ireland, where I've lived for fifty years, bursts with objects from remote times and remote places. Consider my mother's doll – restored and slightly creepy, stranded beneath an elegant bell jar – a gift from my cousin, who found her in our grandmother's shed and brought her to the Doll's Hospital in Dallas. Poor Doll – her name forgotten – peers down from the top of the corner cabinet, itself an antique my children won't want, or rather, have room for.

My husband's great-great-(great?) Grandmother's portrait commands the alcove in the dining room. She has a knowing, challenging look. Where will she go from here? Nobody likes her except me. And then there's Lambie, my own threadbare, bow-legged black sheep. Lambie and I arrived in Ireland together in 1969, when we were both twenty-six, brought by my husband, John, along with our first child. Neither John nor I could have imagined then that we wouldn't live forever, and then die the day after forever, at exactly the same time. We're not meant to think anything else, of course, otherwise we mightn't bother. And who could foresee dementia? Thank goodness, we didn't.

I was well into my middle years when my Aunt Susie, who always told the truth, looked into my eyes and said, 'Sheila, getting old is *hard*.' Susie was widowed young, and she took on her husband's business dealings, played golf, swam, and went for walks in the early mornings, all those things we're supposed to do now. She hated feeling frail. She told me family stories when I visited because she said her boys weren't interested in them yet, which wasn't entirely true. Some of my happiest memories are of sitting beside her on her bed, going through boxes of photos and daguerreotypes of sad-faced young women and raffish-looking old men in rusty Dickensian suits. 'Who could *he* be?...' we'd muse. Susie was hoping that some of us would take all this away from her. In fairness, I think she was nearly ninety when she felt age was really starting to cramp her style.

We really do 'internalise ageism', in today's parlance, which makes it sound like something nasty we ate. Frankly? I hated being eighty. I bought cigarettes and smoked them alone behind the house and sulked for Ireland and Texas combined. The most interesting people I know have already negotiated 'eighty' with grace, but I was scared. Wasn't I called 'Pet' in Castle Street, Dalkey, several months ago, by a genuinely nice, friendly, not-that-young person? In a flash, I was like one of those tiny, grizzled, mean little dogs that show their teeth to children. Up till that moment, I had rather thought of myself as – a lynx. A limping lynx, to be sure, but happy to be alive. After Covid, we don't have to be old to feel grateful for that; just thankful, almost abashed, if we and those we love are still untouched by it. The good part of the birthday-shock was the kindness of my children and friends. They brought flowers, and they also brought plants, things to keep growing. It was a reminder that this fractured world is as safe as it can be, with them in it.

When we were vaccinated last year, when we could travel again, I set out to visit my daughter in New York, then old friends and family in Texas. I set out to check if 'home' was really just a time, or still a place as well. There are bits of Texas in me that I've only dimly understood, being gone for so long. Could the very act of leaving my birthplace be the most Irish part of me now?

My brother and sister-in-law brought me to Big Bend, a thousand square miles of National parkland along the curve of the Rio Grande, the last stop between Texas and Mexico. And there it was: the desert. An endless dreamscape of stone and light, crags and gullies, unearthly in its beauty and its sheer indifference, so uncompromising that astronauts were sent there so they'd know what to do on the moon. It is, in a word, uncluttered. That was what I 'recognised' as Texas, though it couldn't have been farther from the comfortable suburb where I grew up. Indeed, alone and on foot in that landscape, I would survive for about ten minutes. At night, before the real moon rose, we saw the whole sweep of the Milky Way. I hadn't seen it in years. Ridiculous: in so many places here in Ireland, it must seem almost close enough to touch.

One day we had a peaceful picnic beside the river, opposite the Santa Elena Pass into Mexico. The cliffs are so forbidding that nobody's bothered to put up a fence. As we drove on to Presidio, I was reminded of how the little border station at Aughnacloy has fared over the years of our trips to

Donegal. At first there was a low, purposeful-looking structure. Then it was burnt. Then there was ever-sinking rubble; finally, every sign of it was gone. It may take far longer for the Texas-Mexican border to soften, but it too is really an artifice: 'El Paso'; 'Presidio'; 'Laredo...' the Spanish names are everywhere. There's even a 'San Patricio de Hibernia'. 'Terlingua' comes from even older, indigenous languages. It became a 'ghost town' after its mines closed in the 1940s, but not everyone left. Its bumpy desert graveyard of sand, stone and scrub is still used and visited. Markers range from low stone structures to higgledy, hand-painted wooden crosses. Inevitably, there are some Irish names among the Spanish ones.

That was last December. This gentle, opalescent morning, I left my brother and sister-in-law to the Air Coach outside Fitzpatrick's Hotel. They've visited here many times, refugees from the Texas summers, and I know to be grateful: never for us, thank goodness, a Texan version of an 'American wake'. A hale-looking man in his sixties was the last to dash to the bus, followed hesitantly by a woman who was nearly caught between the closing doors. There was confusion as he turned to say goodbye to her. The driver, realising she wasn't staying on too, re-opened the doors to release her after their brief last hug and kiss. When she turned to walk back to her car, I saw she was my age and she was crying.

I sat in my car and mourned a little too, for my parents, and all the parents whose children may feel forced to leave, as I never was. Indeed many of the people who cared for my husband so tenderly during his last years left homes half a world away to make their living here.

I've loved Ireland from the outset, never forgetting Texas, but I was never quite contented until now. Perhaps it's neither 'time' nor territory, but shared feelings and simple kindness that make a place 'home'? Getting old, anywhere, is largely a matter of luck; we've always known that, but we don't feel it till we get here, locked on to this fabulous roller coaster with the cracks in it. Our bodies may taunt us, like when we were little children and couldn't reach things, but we explore other things now. Most days, it feels like the best adventure of all.

Katie Donovan

Dancing Queens

(for Catherine Harris)

Hair lemon-washed,
eyelids spangled blue,
we pretended to be older
for the disco doormen
in the Marine Hotel.

Now we stomp its boards
to celebrate our sixties,
a new decade,
just breached.

We shimmy, gyrate,
shake and spin
our mysterious bodies
that have crawled, sailed,
birthed and mourned,
yet in many ways
feel the same.

We spiral back to lost scenes:
singing along
to your sister's Beatles tunes,
infusing *Yesterday*
with every tremolo
of our young throats;
sneaking to the kitchen
for spoonfuls of Horlicks powder,
crackers and butter -
our 'midnight feasts';

laughing,
in hysterical disbelief
at the book
your mother gave you:
The Facts of Life.

'Dancing Queens' (from *May Swim*, Bloodaxe, 2024)

Maria McManus

What Odds

My mother hung up the phone on me. That was the second time in a week. It was the second time in my lifetime.

I don't want to hear from you the rest of this day. Nor tomorrow either. Nor the day after that. This has done me more harm and has taken more out of me than 'the covus' or anything. You're abusing me now. Then she hung up and cut off the call.

I retaliated. I am not proud of that. I did speak back to her, and I was out of order. I ran out of patience. I was also worried. I was also defensive and self-protective.

I refused to go to her.

*

What is all this? Cleaning, cleaning, cleaning? There's other ways to get rid of the 'covus' than cleaning? I will leave this house. I will just pack up and go.

I try to tell her it is not sustainable. That we cannot go in to assist her and to do the things that the carers cannot do. Clean. The laundry. Re-stock the fridge and make sure she has food. The pharmacy run. There is no-one to do these things.

I cannot do these things now. I am too far away to be able to nip in and out. I don't have the vaccine. I don't have the PPE and I don't want to go in there. I don't want to get sick. I am not willing to put myself at risk, especially if instead we can contract the right services to go in.

I am sick of caring. I have had enough of it. Again and again across the autumn and the winter I dropped everything I was doing. I packed a suitcase and went to sleep on my mother's small sofa in the room next door to hers. I slept in my clothes. An hour here or there. Day was night was day. She'd fractured her arm in a fall, so all personal care, mobilising, getting in and out of bed and the shower and the loo, needed full assistance. She was awake often in the night and needed help with clothes and slippers, meds, the loo – through the infections, the falls, the fractures and dislocations, and the side effects of certain antibiotics. C. Diff. Clostridium Difficile. It's shitty.

When she was vomiting, I cleaned up. When she was incontinent, I cleaned that too. All of it. The underwear and clothes, the bedlinen, and towels. The laundry and the shopping. And the cooking. And the snacks and the tea and the soup and the wee *googy* egg in a cup. I drove her to the monastery when she felt able and needed a run out of the house. We'd go for Mass cards and holy candles, and just for the run.

Fill that bottle with water for me. If I take a fit of coughing in the chapel, I like havin' a drop of water with me. The bottle, carried in her handbag, was hard green semi-transparent plastic with a yellow stopper – a flip top lid, a bit like that on a shampoo bottle. The label had an image of St. Brigid on it and the words, *St. Brigid Protect Our Livestock*. When her 'form' was good we could go a bit further afield. Road trips. Around the countryside, over mountains, beside lakes, through the town, to the pharmacy, the optician, to graveyards, convenience stores, pound shops, the Post Office and supermarkets, the Friary in Rossnowlagh, where she bought industrial quantities of Mass cards, and those holy candles in plastic 'glass' – candles she lit with intention for sick people/ old people/the bereaved/ the expectant/ those doing driving tests/ exams/ people waiting on medical test results/ people waiting to die etc. She lit candles and set them in the kitchen sink in case she'd forget to blow them out.

We went to Rossnowlagh for the day. It was August. The rain was torrential, the beach totally deserted but for an ice-cream van with its prinking music – the theme music to Grandstand, if you must know.

'*Holy God*', she said about the rain. I needed the windscreen wipers on as fast as they'd go, just so we could see out. The sea and sky merged in blurry thundering grey. We decided against getting ice-cream. *Blood sugars 1, ice-cream, nil.*

She couldn't hear well anymore and lost her hearing aid in a supermarket, *foothering with a face mask*. Unlike me, she could use the multiple remote controls for TV and digital stations, and though she was oblivious to the loudness of the radio/TV/iPhone/iPad, she surfed 'the net', kept up with all news on Facebook and played endless games of Solitaire and Candy Crush. She could track down Mass online in the local chapel, but also, in any language at any time of the night or day, when she felt like it – if it looked like Mass, and had the right choreography and cadence, Mass was Mass, even in Latin American Spanish at 3.00 a.m. though she didn't speak Spanish. '*Ach, what odds, Mass is Mass.*'

In the small hours of the morning, she lay up on her big bed, propped up on a whean of pink pillows. The essential supplies she needed to hand were her rosary beads, glasses, hearing aid, a glass of water, tissues, her inhaler, multiple remote controls, her iPad and her phone. Bin and slippers were beside the bed, ready for action when necessary.

I just wanna dance with you, sang Daniel O'Donnell. Nathan Carter begged his mamma to rock him like an interminable-fucking-wagon wheel. She streamed country music through her iPad. She prayed. She snored. She coughed.

I recorded a sample of the channel surfing; a single one minute twenty second recording includes:

Football match commentary, *Watkins, Grealish, Waat-kinns!* (stadium crowd sounds)/

A woman's voice, English, *the luxury; we, we, we need sleep... it /*

A deep and throaty American voice, underscored by dramatic, cinematic music...*Steen....he robs, kills./*

A young, American female, *I guess that what it was, was that I didn't want to be alone over the holidays and I thought that if I was somewhere else I'd reali.../*

Gruff older male, guffawing at a younger man who says, 'he assaulted *me* and he's accusing *us* of being blokey or laddish/

Full blast of Queen and Freddie Mercury, *No, no, no, no, there's no stopping meeeee/*

Jazz or swing orchestra playing a 20's style American waltz /

I thought she'd stick with the swing band, but she flicked on to some melancholic orchestral music. She tolerated about five bars of that, then silence. At last, there was silence.

*

There were shopping channels and game shows, and cookery demonstrations. There was Mass in any language you care to mention, at any time of the night or day. There were homes under the hammer, places in the sun, Lalique collectables on The Antique's Road Show, cash in the attic, Gogglebox, Strictly Come Dancing and Ant and Dec with a lot of desperate celebrities holed up somewhere in Wales goading each other.

There were mice in the ceiling, galloping down the rafters between the houses in this long, long terrace. Pest control did come. Despite the pandemic – the pest control man came. Eventually we were also lucky that several months in, there was a transition and carers were in place. Hospital was avoided.

We were all relieved when she got the Covid vaccine. And we were all dismayed when she, and my sister, came down with Covid, within days of our mother receiving her first vaccine. Each of them sick within days of each other.

At first, I assumed that receiving the news that mother has tested positive for Covid was all that was necessary for it to be understood we were in new territory; she would have to isolate, bar the presence of carers and that my role would be emotional support and contact via phone, FaceTime.

But the message was that it was *handy that there were other rooms in the house, because 'someone' could just stay there and be upstairs.* This was a recurrent message, over a day or two.

I was in denial – I didn't believe that I would be expected to provide 'business as usual' if/when Covid came into the house. I think I expected it to be understood that it would be a game-changer, entirely.

Me: *I need to get advice. I need to check the regulations. I don't have the right PPE. I don't have the vaccine. This is so contagious it isn't possible to be there and not get it.* I would be far away from home, sick and no-one to take care of me.

And why would you be any different from these girls coming in here? my mother asked me. *XX says, that you could come here for three or four days, and you can just stay up the stairs.*

I can't. She's wrong and you are wrong. I can't just come and stay. Not now. This is what is different; Covid is not like the other infections, nor the falls, nor the fractures and it's not the flu. It is not the same. This is what we have talked about all along in the context of the pandemic – that if it hit, we needed to have a plan in place to make sure you would have care, meaning care services because we cannot be there.

Well, at least XX cares about me. The inference being that I clearly didn't.

I do care about you, and you know full well that every other time when you have been ill or needed something, I have dropped what I am doing, and I have gone there. I did whatever was needed. I care and I showed I care. And this is not like the other times. Decisions now about what to do is not like the other times.

The carers have the right PPE, the right protective gear. They have the vaccine. There is a service and if one can't come, another will. If I go there, I don't have PPE, I don't have the vaccine. Just by being there it means I can't go home for at least 17 days.'

What function would I have there – to check the food supplies and the pharmacy supplies? It wouldn't change anything – one more person locked in the house and unable to do the things that need done outside the house.

And the inevitable happened.

She was ill, and alone and frightened of dying. And the rules of engagement had changed.

She said, *They bury people in body bags.* She said this repeatedly. *They put people in body bags and put them in coffins.*

I don't like it that I failed to find a way to go there then to stay with my sick, frail, vulnerable, stubborn, feisty 85-year-old mother. I hit a limit in myself that I don't like. It doesn't sit easily with me, but I didn't go.

I was broken. Exhausted. And full of rage.

Ivy Bannister

I'll Pass

No thanks. Not me. I don't believe I shall.
The time isn't ripe, not just now, when
there's Japanese to learn and the piccolo
to play, and each dot to mull over
in the paintings of Seurat. I don't like
funerals; too often they're grim. Who
wants to be buried in tandem with worms?
Since life's such a joy, all I want is more.
I'm not *that* old. My mind is frisky.
I lift weights, I do yoga and dying's not
pretty – good God! – it might hurt, so
the bottom line reads: I refuse to do it.
Not now. Not ever. No way. I won't.

Contributor Biographies

IVY BANNISTER was born in New York City in 1951. In 1970, she came to Ireland to study at Trinity College, Dublin, where she earned her Ph.D. Her books are: *Blunt Trauma*, a memoir; *Vinegar and Spit*, poetry; and *Magician*, short stories. Several plays have been broadcast by RTÉ radio, and she has written more than fifty pieces for Sunday Miscellany and The Living Word. Awards include the Francis MacManus and Hennessy for fiction, and the O.Z. Whitehead, Listowel, and Mobil Ireland for stage plays. Amongst her poetry awards are Best Small Collection Listowel, the Kilkenny Prize and the Kent and Sussex.

SHEILA (McKee) BARRETT was born in Dallas, Texas, in 1943. She moved to Ireland with her husband, John Barrett, in 1969. Her first short story, 'Advent Rites', was published by Arlen House in their third competition collection, *The Adultery*, in 1982. Subsequent stories have been anthologised or broadcast on radio. Her most recent story is 'Anne and the Indian Princess', in *Tearing Stripes off Zebras*. Her two novels are *Walk in a Lost Landscape* and *A View to Die For*, published by Poolbeg.

MARY ROSE CALLAGHAN was born in Dublin in 1944. A winner in the first Arlen House short story competition, her first novel, *Mothers*, was published as a result. She went on to write ten more novels, two of which were translated into German and Danish. A biography of Kitty O'Shea was a bestseller. Her play, *A House for Fools*, was performed and she has had poetry in the popular *Washing Windows* series, published by Arlen House, also publishers of *Awkward Women* (2022). *The Deep End*, a memoir, was published in the US in 2016.

EILEEN CASEY was born in County Offaly in 1956. She is Hennessy Award Winner (Emerging Fiction) and Patrick and Katherine Kavanagh Fellowship recipient; her poetry and prose are widely published in anthologies by Arlen House, New Island, Faber & Faber, *The Nordic Irish Studies Journal, Poetry Ireland Review*, among others. Her most recent collection *Bog Treasure* (Arlen House, 2021) is a poetry collaboration between Eileen Casey and Canadian Visual Artist Jeanne Cannizzo. A regular contributor to *Senior Times*, she received the Individual Artist Bursary, 2023, from South County Dublin Arts, to complete a poetry collection on the subject of ageing. Supported by County Offaly Arts, she collaborated on a number of commissions.

EVELYN CONLON – described as 'one of Ireland's major truly creative writers' – is a novelist, short story writer, radio essayist, and compiler of anthologies. Born in 1952, her work is poetic, ascerbic, spare and beautifully descriptive. Books include *My Head is Opening, Taking Scarlet as a Real Colour, Stars in the Daytime, Not the Same Sky*, among several others. Her latest books are *Moving About the Place* (2021) a collection of short stories, and a collection of essays, *Reading Rites: Books, writing and Other Things that Matter* (2023). She lectures in Creative Writing and is a member of Aosdána. *Telling Truths: Evelyn Conlon And The Task of Writing*, Peter Lang, 2023, was edited by Teresa Caneda-Cabrera.

TRICIA CRONIN was born in London of Kerry parents in 1953 and now lives in Kerry near one of her daughters and a Kerry-born granddaughter. Her three children completed third level education in Dublin and, although born in London, all three identify as Irish rather than English – their father's family background was Cork and Limerick. Her son now lives in Italy, and the youngest daughter on the south coast of England. She participated in the 'Restorying Ageing' workshop in 2022, and the memoir was written during that workshop.

CELIA DE FRÉINE was born in Newtownards, Co. Down, in 1948. She is an award-winning author who writes in many genres in Irish and English. Her YA novel *An Dara Rogha* (LeabhairCOMHAR, 2021) has been compared to the work of Atwood and Orwell. *Aoi ag Bord na Teanga* (new and selected poems) and *Leanaí Séanta* (a collection of plays) were published by *Leabhair*COMHAR in 2022 and 2023 respectively.

KATHRYN DAILY is a US American living in Donegal. In 2001, she won the Charles Macklin Poetry Competition. Her collection of poetry *The Comfort of a Wicked Past* (Summer Palace Press) was published in 2008. Her poetry has also been included in *Crannóg, Stony Thursday, Landing Places: Immigrant Poets in Ireland* (Dedalus Press), and in other Irish literary collections and journals, both in English and in translation as Gaeilge. She participated in the 'Restorying Ageing' workshop in 2022.

MOYRA DONALDSON was born in 1956. She has published ten collections of poetry, her work is widely anthologised and she has read at festivals in Europe, Canada and America. In 2019, she received a Major Individual Artist award from the Arts Council of Northern Ireland. Her latest collection, *Bone House*, was published by Doire Press 2021.

KATIE DONOVAN was born in 1962 and spent her youth on a farm near Camolin in Co. Wexford. She studied at Trinity College Dublin and at the University of California at Berkeley. She spent a year teaching English in Hungary, 1987-1988. She moved back to Dublin where she worked for *The Irish Times* for 13 years as a journalist in the Features Dept. Her books of poetry have all been published by Bloodaxe Books. *Off Duty* was shortlisted for the Irish Times/Poetry Now Prize in 2017, and in that year she also received the O'Shaughnessy Award for Irish Poetry. Her sixth collection, *May Swim*, was published in May of 2024.

MARY DORCEY was born in 1950. Her work is taught and researched in universities from North America to Europe, China and Africa. She won the Rooney Prize for Irish Literature in 1990 for her short fiction collection, *A Noise from the Woodshed*. Her novel, *Biography of Desire*, has been both a bestseller, having been reprinted three times, and achieved critical acclaim. She has published nine books, three of fiction and six of poetry, all from Salmon Poetry. She was the first woman in Irish history to campaign publicly for LGBT rights and the first to address the subject openly in literature. A lifelong feminist and gay rights activist, she was a founder member of Irishwomen United in 1975 and Women for Radical Change in 1973. She is a Research Associate at Trinity College Dublin where she led seminars on women's literature and led creative writing workshops for many years. She is currently at work on a new novel. In 2010 Mary was elected to the Irish Academy of writers and artists, Aosdána.

CATHERINE DUNNE was born in 1954. She is the author of twelve novels, one work of non-fiction, and several essays. Her work has been translated into a dozen languages and shortlisted for a number of prizes, including Novel of the Year at the Irish Book awards and the International Strega Prize. Her ninth novel, *The Things We Know Now*, won the Giovanni Boccaccio International Prize for Fiction in 2013. *The Years That Followed*, published in 2016, was longlisted for the International Dublin Literary Award. Her latest, *A Good Enough Mother*, won the inaugural Rapallo BPER Banca Prize for fiction in 2023. She is a member of Aosdána.

ANNE GRIFFIN was born in Dublin in 1969. She is the author of *The Island of Longing*, *Listening Still* and *When All Is Said*. Winner of the Irish Book Awards Newcomer of the Year 2019, shortlisted for the John McGahern Annual Book prize and longlisted for the Dublin Literary Award, Anne's work is published in twenty-five territories.

KERRY HARDIE ninth collection *We Go On* was published by Bloodaxe Books in February 2024, following two other Bloodaxe publications, *Where Now Begins* (2020) and *The Zebra Stood in the Night*. Six earlier collections have been published by the Gallery Press and a *Selected Poems* was co-published with Bloodaxe Books. Her work has been widely translated and anthologized and has won many prizes and awards. She has also written two novels [Harper Collins; Little, Brown], and a radio play (RTE). She has just completed another novel. She lives in Kilkenny with her husband Seán.

PHYL HERBERT is a Dubliner. After a career in teaching and theatre she addressed the writing side of her life. In 2008 she qualified with an M.Phil in Creative writing in Trinity College. Her debut collection of short stories *The Price of Desire* was published by Arlen House in 2016 and her essay 'The Fruit of a Life' was published by Arlen House in *Look! It's a Woman Writer* (ed. Éilís Ní Dhuibhne) in 2021. Her memoir, *The Price of Silence*, was published in 2023 by Menma Books.

RITA ANN HIGGINS was born in Galway in 1955. *Pathogens Love a Patsy (Pandemic and other Poems)*, published by Salmon Press in 2020, is her eleventh book of poetry. In 2020 Rita Ann became the People's Pandemic Poet for The Brendan O'Connor Show on RTE Radio 1. Bloodaxe Books has published several of her collections including *Throw in the Vowels: New and Selected Poems* (2005) and *Ireland is Changing Mother* (2011/14), and *Tongulish* (2016). She has written several plays. In 2021 she received The Living Poets Society Award. She is a member of Aosdána.

SOPHIA HILLAN, born in 1950, is former Associate Director of Queen's University Belfast's Institute of Irish Studies (1993-2003) and Director of QUB's Irish Studies Summer School (2003-2005). She is the author of *May, Lou and Cass: Jane Austen's Nieces in Ireland* (2011); of two novels, *The Friday Tree* (2014) and *The Way We Danced* (2016), and a short story collection, *The Cocktail Hour* (2018). She is joint Literary Executor of the estate of Michael McLaverty. Her studies of his work include *The Silken Twine* (1992), *The Edge of Dark* (2000) and (as editor) *In Quiet Places* (1989).

ANN INGLE was born in London in 1939. She moved to Dublin in 1961 having met and married an Irish man, Peter, and they had a family of eight. Peter died in 1980. Ann graduated from Trinity College as a mature student when she was in her 50s. She was asked to ghostwrite the story of Rosemary Smith, the legendary Irish racing driver, and *Driven* was published by Harper Collins in 2018. Ann was 82 when her memoir *Openhearted*, written during lockdown, was published by Penguin Ireland in September 2021.

HEATHER INGMAN, born 1953, is retired Adjunct Professor in the School of English, Trinity College, the University of Dublin. Her publications include *Elizabeth Bowen* (2021), *Strangers to Themselves: Ageing in Irish Writing* (2018), *Irish Women's Fiction from Edgeworth to Enright* (2013), and *A History of the Irish Short Story* (2009). She is co-editor, with Clíona Ó Gallchoir, of *A History of Modern Irish Women's Literature* (2018).

ARJA KAJERMO was born in Finland in 1949 and grew up in Sweden. She has lived in Ireland most of her life. Her cartoons were first published in *The Dublin Magazine* and have featured in numerous Irish publications as well as in the Swedish daily *Dagens Nyheter*. She was one of the six finalists for the Davy Byrnes Short Story Award 2014. Her debut novel *The Iron Age* was published by Tramp Press (2017).

JESSIE LENDENNIE is the founder, co-director and Managing Editor of Salmon Poetry. She was born in Blytheville, Arkansas. For Salmon Poetry, she has commissioned and published over 600 volumes of poetry as well as a select list of literary criticism, drama, fiction, memoir and essays. Her own publications include a book-length prose poem *Daughter* (1988), reprinted as *Daughter and Other Poems* in 2001, and a collection of poetry, *Walking Here* (2011). She compiled and edited: *The Salmon Guide to Creative Writing in Ireland* (1990); *Salmon: A Journey in Poetry 1981-2007* (2007); *Poetry: Reading it, Writing it, Publishing it* (2009); *Dogs Singing: A Tribute Anthology* (2010); and *Even the Daybreak: 35 Years of Salmon Poetry* (2016). In 2021, she was presented with *Days of Clear Light: A Festschrift in Honour of Jessie Lendennie and in Celebration of Salmon at 40*. Edited in secret by Alan Hayes and Nessa O'Mahony, it includes a foreword by President of Ireland Michael D. Higgins and contributions from over 100 poets and members of the wider literary community.

LIZ McMANUS was born in Canada in 1947. She has worked as an architect in Derry, Galway, Dublin and Wicklow, and as a newspaper columnist from 1985-1993. Her first novel *Acts of Subversion* (1991) was shortlisted for the Aer Lingus/ Irish Times award for New Writing. She was awarded a Hennessy New Irish Writing award, Listowel Short Story Award and Irish PEN award. She was conferred with an MPhil in Creative Writing (with distinction), at Trinity College Dublin, in 2012. Her second novel, *A Shadow in the Yard*, was published in 2015, and a third, *When Things Come to Light*, in 2023. A parliamentarian for 19 years, she was Minister for Housing and Urban Renewal (1994-97) and is a former chairperson of the Board of the Irish Writers Centre.

MARIA McMANUS was born in Enniskillen in 1964. Her poetry collections are *Available Light* (Arlen House), *We Are Bone*, *The Cello Suites* and *Reading the Dog* (Lagan Press). *Ellipses* is published as a limited-edition hand-made pamphlet (Coast to Coast to Coast, 2021).

Collaborations for choral, wind and string ensembles include ELLIPSES, An Anthem to End Wars, and WRETCHES, with Keith Acheson, and Tierra Sallada with Martin Devek. Her work has been broadcast on RTE, BBC Radio and BBC World Service. Maria is a founding artistic director of Quotidian – Word on the Street, which includes the Poetry Jukebox.

TERESA MASON was born in 1971. She is an occupational therapist and group analyst living in Co. Tipperary. Teresa participated in the 'Restorying Ageing' workshop in 2022 and is grateful to have learned a lot from all the women involved in the initiative. She was recently awarded a PhD by TUS for a thesis which was her psychosocial exploration of the importance of the symbol of Sheela-na-gig to contemporary Ireland.

PAULA MEEHAN, born in Dublin in 1955, has received both critical and popular acclaim for her work, winning many prizes and being honoured with election to Aosdána in 1996. She is an Honorary Fellow of Trinity College Dublin, she is an alumnus of Eastern Washington University, (MFA 1983), she has an Honorary Doctorate from Dublin City University and is an Honorary Fellow of the Royal Hibernian Academy. She was Ireland Professor of Poetry (2013-2016). *As If By Magic: Selected Poems*, 2020, and *The Solace of Artemis*, 2023, were both published by Dedalus Press, Dublin.

LIA MILLS was born in Dublin in 1957. She writes novels, short stories, literary essays, and memoir. Her novel, *Fallen*, was the Dublin/Belfast Two Cities One Book selection in 2016. A new edition of her first novel, *Another Alice*, was published in 2022 as part of the Arlen House Classic Literature series. A Mentor on the National Mentoring Programme, she is currently working on her fourth novel.

CAROLINE MORAN, born in 1969, lives in the West of Ireland with her husband and four children. The 'Restorying Ageing' workshop in 2022 was her first attempt at creative writing. She found the experience to be both terrifying and exhilarating.

MARY MORRISSY (b 1957) is the author of four novels, *Mother of Pearl*, *The Pretender*, *The Rising of Bella Casey* and most recently, *Penelope Unbound*, a speculative novel about Nora Barnacle. Her short fiction has been anthologised widely and she has published two collections of stories, *A Lazy Eye* and *Prosperity Drive*. Her work has won her the Hennessy Prize and a Lannan Foundation Award. A member of Aosdána, she is a journalist, teacher of creative writing and a literary mentor. She blogs at https://marymorrissy.com/ and curates a website on the Dublin painter, Una Watters – https://unawattersartist.com.

ÁINE MOYNIHAN's poetry collection *Canals of Memory* was funded by an Arts Council bursary and appeared under the Doghouse imprint in 2008. That year also saw the opening of An Lab, the Irish language theatre and arts centre in Dingle which she founded and managed for a decade. In the past year she wrote and performed a bi-lingual one-woman show called *Feisteas an tSaoil/Dressing the Part*.

MEADHBH Ni BHRADAIGH was born in Granard in 1942, where she still lives and where she worked as a teacher and later as a Community Worker in Rath Mhuire and Dolmen Failte Group in North Longford. She has been involved with Granard Writer's Group since its inception in 1987. She released a video on YouTube 'A Time to Remember, journey of reconciliation' to mark 100 years since the struggle for independence in Longford. She participated in the 'Restorying Ageing' workshop in 2022.

ÉILÍS NÍ DHUIBHNE was born in Dublin in 1954. She has published many collections of short stories, novels, books for children, in both Irish and English. She is a literary critic and facilitated the creative writing 'Restorying Ageing' workshop in 2022. She is a member of Aosdána and President of The Folklore of Ireland Society.

HELENA NOLAN was born in Thomastown, Co. Kilkenny, in 1966. She is a graduate of the MA in Creative Writing in UCD. Her poetry has been widely published and has won awards including the Patrick Kavanagh Award. A diplomat for many years, she is currently the Irish Consul General in New York. She edited, with colleagues Ragnar Almqvist and Angela Byrne, an anthology of writing by Irish diplomats, *All Strangers Here*, published by Arlen House in 2022.

BRIGID O'BRIEN loves to draw. She uses pen, pencil and watercolour to create pictures of people on trains, in cafés, and on beaches.

JEAN O'BRIEN, born in Dublin in 1952, is an award-winning poet whose sixth collection, *Stars Burn Regardless* was published by Salmon Poetry in 2022. She was a resident at the Centre Culturel Irlandais in Paris in 2021 and was awarded a Kavanagh Fellowship in 2017/18. She teaches creative writing in the Irish Writers Centre and on the MFA for Pittsburgh college. She holds an M.Phil from Trinity College, Dublin.

MARY O'DONNELL is a poet, novelist, short story writer, essayist and lecturer. She has published eight poetry collections including *Massacre of the Birds* (Salmon Poetry, 2020, translated and published in Brazil as *Onde Estou Os Pássaros* in 2023), as well as four novels and three short story collections. Her short fiction is widely anthologised, most recently in the OUP collection *Dublin Tales*. Novels include *The Light Makers* (1992, 1993, 2018) *The Elysium Testament* (1999), and *Where They Lie* (2014). Her poetry chapbook *Outsiders, Always* was published by Southword in 2023. Her work can be viewed on the Poetry Foundation's website as well as on Poetry International (NL). As a teacher of creative writing, her interest is in the forms, practices and critical reception of contemporary literature. She is a member of the artists' affiliation Aosdána. www.maryodonnell.com

ROSE O'DRISCOLL, born in 1955, is a feminist sociologist who has taught at undergraduate and postgraduate levels at universities in the UK and Ireland. Prior to entering academia Rose worked as a practitioner and manager in the Third sector in Ireland, England and Wales. She is also a Senior Fellow of the Higher Education Academy. Rose, now retired, has returned to live in the area in which she grew up. As a fledgling creative writer, Rose is interested in exploring the lives of older rural women in west Cork. In particular, the lives of women who bucked the system and did their own thing. She was a participant in the 'Restorying Ageing' workshop in 2022.

NESSA O'MAHONY was born in Dublin. She has published five books of poetry – *Bar Talk* (1999), *Trapping a Ghost* (2005), *In Sight of Home* (2009), *Her Father's Daughter* (2014) and *The Hollow Woman on the Island* (2019). She has edited journals and anthologies and writes fiction and non-fiction.

MARY RAFFERTY trained as a Speech and Language Therapist and went on to work in research, training and organisation development. In her later life she is enjoying discovering the unexplored parts of her creativity and is now busy making artist's books, cyanotpe prints, collages and paste papers. She loves words and language and is an occasional poet. She is now learning how to play. Mary lives in Dublin, but will travel for play. She was a participant in the 'Re-storying Ageing' workshop in 2022.

ÁINE RYAN is an award-winning journalist who has written widely about Clare Island, Co Mayo. From Dublin originally, she lived on the island for 16 years and returns regularly these days from her home in Westport. Her articles and essays have appeared in many newspapers over the years and she is a regular contributor to the *Irish Times*.

MICHAELA SCHRAGE-FRÜH is Associate Professor in German Studies at the University of Limerick. She is co-founder of the Women and Ageing Research Network and was Principal Investigator of the Irish Research Council-funded project 'Restorying Ageing: Older Women and Life Writing' (2021-2022).

LORNA SHAUGHNESSY, born in 1961, has published four poetry collections with Salmon Poetry: *Torching the Brown River, Witness Trees, Anchored* and, most recently, *Lark Water* (2023) as well as a chapbook with Lapwing Press, *Song of the Forgotten Shulamite*. She has translated four volumes of Mexican and Spanish poetry and co-edited *A Different Eden. Ecopoetry from Ireland and Galicia* (Dedalus 2021). www.lornashaughnessy.com

AILBHE SMYTH, born in Dublin in 1946, the founding head of Women's Studies at UCD, Ailbhe Smyth has published widely on feminism, sexuality and reproductive issues. She is a long-time feminist, LGBTIQ+ and socialist activist and played a leading role in the Irish referendums on marriage equality and abortion. She is a director of Age Action Ireland, Patron of the Women's Collective Ireland, Chair of Women's Aid, and also of Ballyfermot STAR Addiction Services. In 2019, she was included in *Time Magazine*'s '100 Most Influential People' list. She was awarded an Honorary Doctorate in Laws by the University of Galway, and was conferred with the Freedom of the City of Dublin in 2022.

MÁIRÍDE WOODS writes poetry and short stories. Her work has appeared in anthologies and reviews and has been broadcast on RTE radio. She has won several prizes, including two Hennessy awards, the Francis McManus and PJ O'Connor awards from RTE. Three poetry collections, including *A Constant Elsewhere of the Mind* (2017), have been published by Astrolabe. One of her essays appeared in *Look! It's a Woman Writer* (2022). Máiríde was brought up in County Antrim but has lived most of her life in North Dublin.

Acknowledgments

This anthology wouldn't have been possible without the support of various people and institutions. The book is one of the outputs of the research project 'Restorying Ageing: Older Women and Life Writing' (2021-2022). We gratefully acknowledge the generous funding received by the Irish Research Council under the New Foundations Scheme (2021) as well as by the University of Galway under the CASSCS Strategic Research Development Scheme (2022/23).

We would like to thank Age & Opportunity, our partner in the 'Restorying Ageing' project, specifically Mary Harkin, Dr Tara Byrne, and Eva Griffin, as well as the members of the Age & Opportunity PPI group for their invaluable input. Some of the poems included here resulted from a 'Restorying Ageing' creative life writing workshop, led by Éilís Ní Dhuibhne and co-organised with Age & Opportunity, and were first presented at the 'Restorying Ageing' webinar as part of the Bealtaine festival 2022.

We would like to sincerely thank our 'Restorying Ageing' project collaborators Dr Margaret O'Neill and Karen Hanrahan. Most of all, we would like to express our heartfelt gratitude to all the women participating in the focus group and creative life writing sessions and to all writers sharing their reflections on ageing as part of this anthology.

MICHAELA SCHRAGE-FRÜH & ÉILÍS NÍ DHUIBHNE

SALMON

'Publishing the finest Irish and international literature.'

MICHAEL D. HIGGINS, President of Ireland